WORKING WAGONS

A pictorial review of freight stock
on the B.R. system.

by

David Larkin

Volume 3. 1980 to 1984

Santona Publications
Hull

Working Wagons

Volume 3. 1980 - 1984

First Published 2001

British Library Cataloguing-in-publication Data.
A catalogue record for this book is available from the British Library

First Published in 2001 by;
Santona Publications,
Rydal Mount,
224, Marlborough Avenue,
Hull. HU5 3LE.

Design & typesetting by Santona Publications.
Photographic printing by Steve Flint Photography, Hull.
Printed by The Amadeus Press Ltd.

ISBN 0 9538448 2 X.

WORKING WAGONS

Volume 3. 1980 - 1984

Contents

Introduction		Page 5
T.O.P.S. Codes		Page 8
Section 1	16T Mineral Wagons	Page 10
Section 2	21T Mineral Wagons	Page 12
Section 3	Iron Ore Tippler Wagons	Page 14
Section 4	Highfit Wagons	Page 16
Section 5	B.R. 25.5T Hoppers	Page 18
Section 6	B.R. Presflo Wagons	Page 20
Section 7	B.R. Covhop Wagons	Page 22
Section 8	4 wheeled Steel Wagons (Traditional)	Page 24
Section 9	Bogie Bolster C and D (VB types)	Page 26
Section 10	Other Bogie Steel Wagons (Traditional)	Page 28
Section 11	Boplate Wagons and Variations	Page 30
Section 12	Strip Coil Wagons	Page 32
Section 13	Lowmac and Rectank Wagons	Page 34
Section 14	Brake Vans	Page 36
Section 15	Early Air Braked Wagons	Page 38
Section 16	Air Braked Open Wagons	Page 40
Section 17	Air Braked Vans (VDA)	Page 42
Section 18	Other Air Braked Vans	Page 44
Section 19	B.R. Ferry Vans	Page 46
Section 20	Air Braked Bogie Bolster (BDA)	Page 48
Section 21	Bogie Steel AB (BAA etc.)	Page 50

Contents
(continued)

Section 22	Air Braked Steel Wagons (Other)	Page 52
Section 23	HAA Hoppers and Variants	Page 54
Section 24	4 wheeled Scrap Wagons	Page 56
Section 25	Private Owner Open and Steel Wagons	Page 58
Section 26	Private Owner Bogie Tippler Wagons	Page 60
Section 27	Private Owner 4 wheeled Hoppers	Page 62
Section 28	Private Owner 4 wheeled Covhops	Page 64
Section 29	Private Owner Bogie Covhops (1)	Page 66
Section 30	Private Owner Bogie Covhops (2)	Page 68
Section 31	Private Owner 4 wheeled Powder (APCM)	Page 70
Section 32	Private Owner 4 wheeled Powder (Other)	Page 72
Section 33	Private Owner Railtanks (Shell Mex and B.P. - 1)	Page 74
Section 34	Private Owner Railtanks (Shell Mex and B.P. - 2)	Page 76
Section 35	Private Owner Railtanks (Other - 1)	Page 78
Section 36	Private Owner Railtanks (Other - 2)	Page 80
Section 37	Private Owner Railtanks (Bogie)	Page 82
Section 38	Continental Ferry Vans	Page 84
Section 39	Contnental Ferry Railtanks	Page 86
Section 40	P. W. Hopper Wagons (Traditional)	Page 88
Section 41	P. W. Open and Rail Wagons (Traditional)	Page 90
Section 42	P. W. Open Wagons (Refurbished)	Page 92
Section 43	P. W. Hopper Wagons (Modern)	Page 94

Introduction

The years which are covered in this volume, 1980 to 1984, were very eventful. Taking the traditional fleet first, many of the familiar and ubiquitous types were on their way out. The rebuilt unfitted MCO (below) and the 1950s vintage MDO (bottom) are two such examples and both types were withdrawn soon after.

B89668 (Taken at Burry Port, Summer 1981)
By 7/83, only 40 MCO wagons remained in service and all would have looked like this one, which was built in 1951. Such vehicles were very restricted in area and most were probably in South Wales, as indeed this one is. Livery is rusty Rail Grey with black underframe and white lettering on black panels. (Ref: W9542/DL)

Nevertheless, both the 16T Mineral in vacuum braked form and the 21T Mineral in rebuilt form, would remain in service for a few more years yet.

The rebuilding of mineral wagons of both hoppered and non-hoppered types continued far longer than was necessary and may have been a 'sweetener' for the workforce at places like Shildon wagon works, which closed during the review period. Section 2 deals chiefly with a new MDO type that was built in the late 1970s and had a very short life. Also built in large numbers were HTO and HTV coal hoppers, one of which is illustrated on the next page.

Other traditional types were still seen in significant numbers, but for the last time. Sections 3 to 13 cover those traditional types which flourished during the period and section 14 rounds off the traditional scene with a look at brake vans of the period.

Additionally, there were some traditional types that could still be seen in small numbers, such as the FLV container wagon illustrated on the next page, and other traditional types that were rebuilt or just reallocated to become barrier wagons or runner wagons, such as the timber wagon illustrated on page 7.

Turning now to the B.R. air braked fleet, the period proved very confusing. 1980 saw the design and construction of new vans, open wagons and steel carrying wagons, yet by 1985, many of the latter were being transferred to the civil engineer's fleet. The closure of steel works and the subsequent redundancy of wagons that served them explained

Below. ***B200417 (Taken at Longport, Summer 1980)***
The survival as late as 1980 of a riveted Diagram 1/110 MDO mineral wagon was unusual, but not unique, as such stock and the 16T counterpart were generally withdrawn in preference to welded stock or rebuilt to one form or another. Such paint as still exists is Rail Grey but rust is predominant with white lettering on the remnants of a black panel. (Ref: W9593/DL)

E289245 (Taken at Toton Yard, Summer 1980)
It seems rather incredible that an unfitted wagon at least 35 years old and fitted with oil axleboxes should have been rebuilt by B.R. but such is the case with this example. It would be withdrawn in about four years. Livery is Freight Brown with black underframe and white lettering. (Ref: W8708/DL)

the transfer of such vehicles as the BDA and SPA types, but the additional transfer of modern OAA, OBA and OCA revenue wagons did not appear to make economic sense at that time. With hindsight, of course, the engineers were receiving new air braked engineering designs into their fleet, (see Section 43), and this logically dictated the transfer of only compatible, fully air braked vehicles as well. Thus, with a few notable exceptions, the time honoured cascading of the oldest revenue types into departmental use finally came to an end.

The privately owned fleet continued to expand with many new and interesting types appearing; the scrap wagons in section 24, the covhops in section 28 and the bogie covhops in sections 29 and 30, are a few of my own personal favourites.

Railtanks were still being affected by the oil crisis of the 1970s and the trend was definitely against the 100T bogie types that had proved so popular only a decade earlier. Despite this, some new ones were built (see section 36), but many others were being rebuilt as bogie stone wagons with box bodies (see section 26). The period also saw a new practice to emerge, this involved the sale and transfer of P.O. wagons, originally built for one traffic, onto a new owner for a different traffic.

B530644 (Taken at Brixton, Summer 1980)
The Conflat L was very much a vehicle of the 1950s and they were being withdrawn as early as 1969. It was therefore something of a surprise to see examples of the type still in regular use at the start of the review period. Most of those recorded at this time were carrying doloma to Sheerness steel works. They were in very rusty condition with lots of white powder staining. Lettering was white. (Ref: W8241/DL)

B455524 (Taken at Middlesborough, Autumn 1981)
To convert a timber wagon to a runner, all stanchions were removed and half the end laid flat on the floor (to give extra weight to the vehicle), as seen here. Curiously, although still vacuum braked, it is acting as a runner to two air braked BDA wagons. Livery is rust and weathered wood. (Ref: W10033/DL).

Ferry vehicles were quite numerous but they had yet to take a firm hold on van traffic; they eventually did, however, in grand style in the next review period dealt with in Volume 4. Other new ferry types were appearing, such as the POLYBULK hoppers in section 30 and the railtanks in section 39.

As mentioned above, the civil engineer's fleet was going through a period of great change. Air braked vehicles were being transferred into the fleet and this was to do away with such types as the ZGO below. Vacuum braked designs such as the hopper seen in section 40 were safe for a while but they were not generally given modern brakes as were the rail wagons in section 41. At the start of the review period there were various dabblings with modernising old revenue open wagons, as illustrated in section 42. The next review period saw even further great change in this area and this will be covered in Volume 4.

Also in this period, two significant changes to my own personal approach to the study of wagons occurred.

Firstly, many of the signal boxes in which I had worked were closed due to the commissioning, during the review period, of the Victoria Signalling Centre. This saw the demise of such fruitful locations as Battersea, Brixton and Nunhead. I now had to go further afield to take photographs!

Secondly, I was granted permission to inspect wagon records at B.R. Headquarters in Derby and thus began to acquire the knowledge to back up the photographs. For instance, the totals I have quoted for 7/83 were taken from this source. So many thanks must go to the staff of the old Rolling Stock Library, in particular, to Tom Scrivenor, Gordon Potts, David Munro and Brent Adams, and their lady colleagues as well. Thanks especially for being allowed to use their T.O.P.S. machine to chase down rare wagons, such as ADC920500 on page 38. So, on to Volume 4, which will see much change in the run up to privatisation of B.R.

David Larkin
Sutton, Surrey.
August 2001.

DB483685 (Taken at Normanton, Winter 1980)
Surely the very last appearance of this Diagram 1/033 dropside high, appropriately lettered TO WORK BETWEEN HULL PARAGON STN. AND BARLOW TIP. Such types were swept away during the review period by modern air braked wagons. Livery is grey with black underframe and white lettering. (Ref: W9284/DL)

T.O.P.S. codes

Following on from Volume 2. this section gives further T.O.P.S. codes and the revisions to certain **J-prefixed, K-prefixed, U-prefixed** and **X-prefixed** codes from 1/10/83.

BFV Formerly JZV, Bogie Coil X wagons. B949551 to B949608
BGV Formerly JGV, Bogie Coil G wagons. ex. Warflat
BJV Formerly JEV, Bogie Coil E wagons. ex. Warflat
BNX Formerly JKX, Bogie Coil K wagons. B9495XX series
BUV Formerly JMV, Bogie Coil M wagons. ex. BDVs
BVV Formerly JVV, Bogie Coil V wagons. B949050 to B949089
BWV Formerly JPV, Bogie Coil P wagons. ex. BBEs
BYV Formerly JTV, Bogie Coil T wagons. B9495XX series
HYV Formerly UYV, Anhydrite hoppers. B747000 to B747149
OOV Formerly UCV, China clay wagons in B743XXX range
PAA P.O. 4wh. Covhop. *Air-braked only*
PAB P.O. 4wh. Covhop. *Air-braked & Vacuum-piped*
PAF P.O. 4wh. Covhop. *Vacuum-braked*
PBA P.O. Bogie Covhop. *Air-braked only*
PCA P.O. 4wh. Bulk Powder. *Air-braked only*
PCB P.O. 4wh. Bulk Powder. *Air-braked & Vacuum-piped*
PCF P.O. 4wh. Bulk Powder. *Vacuum-braked*
PCV P.O. 4wh. Bulk Powder. *Vacuum-braked*
PDA P.O. Bogie Bulk Powder. *Air-braked only*
PFA P.O. Flat or Container. *Air-braked only*
PGA P.O. 4wh. Hopper. *Air-braked only*
PHA P.O. Bogie Hopper. *Air-braked only*
PIA P.O. Ferry non-tank. *Air-braked only*
PIB P.O. Ferry non-tank. *Air-braked &Vacuum-piped*
PJB P.O. Cartic-4 set. *Air-braked & Vacuum-piped*
PKA P.O. 3-axle Car. double-deck. *Air-braked only*
PLA P.O. Bogie Car. double-deck. *Air-braked only*
PMA P.O. 4wh. Mineral. *Air-braked only*
PNA P.O. Bogie Open. *Air-braked only*
POA P.O. 4wh. Open. *Air-braked only*
PQA P.O. 3-axle Car. single-deck. *Air-braked only*
PRA P.O. 4wh. Open with hood. *Air-braked only*
PSA P.O. 4wh. Open for salt. *Air-braked only*
PTA P.O. Bogie Tippler. *Air-braked only*
PVA P.O. 4wh. Van. *Air-braked only*
PWA P.O. Bogie Van. *Air-braked only*
PXA P.O. Miscellaneous non-tank types. *Air-braked only*
SCO Formerly KCO, unfitted Pig Coil wagons.
SEV Formerly KEV, vacuum braked Coil E wagons. Ex-Plate VBs
SFV Formerly KAV, B949130 to B949179
SGV Formerly KBV, B949180 to B949219
SHA Formerly KTA, Coil T wagons ex. SAA
SJO Formerly KJO, Coil J wagons ex. iron ore tipplers
SKA Formerly KOA, Wire coil wagons. ex. SAA
SRV Formerly KRV, Coil R wagons. ex. Plate VBs
TB Series P.O. Bogie Railtanks from 70T to 79T G.L.W.
TC Series P.O. Bogie Railtanks from 80T to 89T G.L.W.

B743276 (Taken at Lostwithiel, Summer 1981)
When T.O.P.S. codes were originally issued, the traditional fleet, with all its myriad of variations, was the largest and the codes issued at that time reflected this. By the early 1980s it was no longer necessary to keep many of the early codes. When this photograph was taken, all the CLAY HOOD wagons operating in Cornwall were coded UCV but, in two years, this was changed to OOV. (Ref: W9726/DL)

TD Series P.O. Bogie Railtanks from 90T to 99T G.L.W.
TE Series P.O. Bogie Railtanks from 100T G.L.W.
TI Series P.O. Ferry Railtanks all types
TR Series P.O. 4wh. Railtanks from 20T to 29T G.L.W.
TS Series P.O. 4wh. Railtanks from 30T to 39T G.L.W.
TT Series P.O. 4wh. Railtanks from 40T to 49T G.L.W.
TU Series P.O. 4wh. Railtanks over 50T G.L.W.
ZAA **PIKE** Former SPA wagons in DC46xxxx range
ZAO/ZAV Various types including medium goods & tube wagons
ZBA **CARP** DB988600 27T ballast open wagon built 1983
ZBA **HAKE** Rebuilt ZBO GRAMPUS wagons
ZBA **RUDD** Rebuilt ZBO GRAMPUS & DB972000 to DB972799
ZBO/ZBV **GRAMPUS** Std. B.R. ballast open wagon
ZBV **LAMPREY** Early B.R. ballast open wagon
ZCA **SEAHARE** ZAA PIKE wagons with fixed sides
ZCA **SEAHORSE** Rebuilt ABN vans with ballast open bodywork
ZCA **SOLE** Early B.R. ballast open wagon for Merseyrail area
ZCV **CLAM** Rebuilt HTV chassis from 1989. DB973000 to DB973449
ZCV **CRAB** Rebuilt ZBV LAMPREY with fixed sides
ZCV **PLAICE** Ballast open wagon. DB987101 to DB987305
ZCV **TOPE** DB970000 to DB970059, DB970100 to DB970855
ZDA **BASS** Former OBA and OCA wagons
ZDA **SQUID** Former OAA wagons
ZEA **BREAM** Various 4wh. runner wagons. ex-ABN chassis
ZEV **CATFISH** Std. 19T 4wh. ballast hopper wagon
ZFV **DOGFISH** Std. 24T 4wh. ballast hopper wagon
ZJV **MERMAID** Std. 14T 4wh. side tipping ballast wagon
ZLV **HERRING** Early 4wh. 20T ballast hopper wagon
ZMV **MACKEREL** Early 4wh. 17T ballast hopper wagon
ZUV **SHARK** Std. 4wh. 20T ballast plough braked van
YCA **HALIBUT** 52T Bogie ballast open built 1980. DB981000/1
YCV **TURBOT** 34T Bogie ballast. DB978000 to DB978991
YAA **BRILL** Former BDA wagons
YAO **DOLPHIN** Early 50T Bogie ballast, rail & sleeper wagon
YBA **STURGEON** Std. 50T Bogie ballast, rail & sleeper
YDA **SKATE** Bogie skip wagon. DB997801 to DB997822
YEA **PERCH** C.W.R. wagons. DB979000 to DB979131, DB979400 to DB979411
YEA **PORPOISE** C.W.R. wagons. DB979500 to DB979515
YGB **SEA COW** Std. 40T Bogie ballast hopper. *Air-braked & Vacuum-piped*
YGH **SEA LION** Std. 40T Bogie ballast hopper. *Dual-braked*
YGV **WALRUS** Early 40T Bogie ballast hopper
YHA **WHALE** 50T Bogie ballast hopper. DB982350 to DB982439
YLA **MULLET** Former BRA Bogie rail wagons
YLO **GANE A** Early 40T Bogie rail wagon
YMA **SALMON** Std. 50T Bogie rail wagon
YPA **TENCH** YBA STURGEON wagons for concrete track
YQA **PARR** YLA MULLET wagons for concrete track

230339 (Taken at Rochester 07/7/84)
The origin of some of the T.O.P.S. codes is rather obscure. Vanwides were given the logical VWV code when in original condition but those fitted with roller bearings received VEV codes. This was the next vacant code in the air-braked range (such stock normally being given the early letters in the alphabet) and it would appear that the scheme to refurbish thes vehicles with air braking had already been approved. This van is painted in the Grey/Flame Red livery but has weathered such that the red upper band has virtually disappeared. (Ref: W14018/DL)

Section 1. 16T Mineral Wagons

B596256 (Taken at Silvertown, London E, Summer 1980)
The 10' 0" wheelbase vehicles were the only MCV wagons to have roller bearings officially, although the odd one with a 9' 0" wheelbase was recorded. The vacuum-braked vehicles were by far the most numerous in service during the review period but note the MCOs in the right background. Livery is Freight Brown with black underframe and white lettering (Ref. W8468/DL)

We start our review of period three, 1980 to 1984, as we have done with the two previous volumes in this series, with a further look at the 16T all-steel mineral wagon.

Although, as can be seen opposite (top), there were unfitted examples running at the start of the review period, almost all the vehicles recorded were vacuum braked.

These fell within specific number ranges as follows: B126400 to B126499, B229230 to B229251 (9' 0" w.b. with Westinghouse b/gear) B68900 to B68999, B159892 to B160571, B261309 to B261508, B266209 to B266808, B550000 to B550499, B551600 to B552949, B554430 to B554899, B555250 to B555749, B556050 to B557049, B557750 to B558749, B587300 to B590299, B592200 to B592699, B592850 to B593199, B594200 to B594349, B595150 to B595499 (9' 0" w.b. with clasp brakegear), B560200 to B583299 (9' 0" w.b. with push brakegear), B596000 to B596393 (10' 0" w.b. with various brakegear). B555555 (opposite centre) had the most common type of brakegear. B126467 (opposite lower) illustrates the rare Westinghouse type. Nearly all the vehicles from these batches were rebodied; note the wide spread in number blocks and the buffer variations.

Finally, B596256 (above) is an example of the 10' 0" wheelbase batch.

B583427 (Taken at Ellesmere Port, 13/2/82)
The survival of any unfitted 16T mineral wagons into the 1980s still in traffic use was very rare, especially one with original bodywork. This one, I suspect, is in use as a barrier wagon, probably on short trips in the local area where the incompatability of brake types would not be a problem. (Ref: W10514/DL)

Centre. ***B555555(Taken at Hoo Junction, Spring 1981)***
The vacuum-braked 16T minerals were fitted with whatever modern buffer was in fashion at the time of building. This did not change at the time when the wagon was rebuilt. Livery is Freight Brown with black underframe and white lettering. (Ref: W9574/DL)

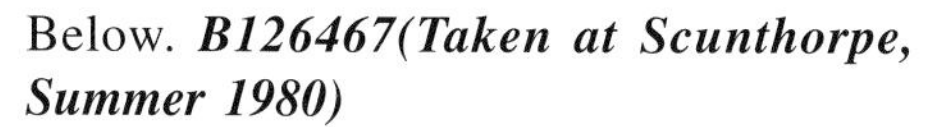

Below. ***B126467(Taken at Scunthorpe, Summer 1980)***
The survival of such rare 16T mineral variants as the one shown here was rather surprising. It had been built back in the early 1950s to work in a test train and had special Westinghouse brakegear. The differences are well worth noting. These also had 1' 6" length OLEO buffers as well. Livery is as above. (Ref: W8371/DL)

Section 2. 21T Mineral Wagons

B316809 (Taken at Longport, Summer 1980)
The first batch of 21T Mineral rebodied stock, as featured in Vol. 2, section 4, were still to be seen at the start of the review period but were being broken up by the end of the period. B316809 is one of the rarer examples, using the chassis from a L.N.E.R. 21T coal hopper, which has brake shoes on one side only. Livery is Rail Grey with black underframe and white lettering on black panels. (Ref: W8066/DL)

Somewhat surprisingly, B.R. decided to pursue the rebuilding of various vehicles to MDO type, although they had already done 2500 such vehicles (see above and Vol. 2, section 4. for details).

The new fleet also involved the fitting of heavier springs and uprating from 21.5T to 25T, making the choosing of numbers for modelling purposes rather difficult.

The common feature to the new design was the bodywork. This had no end doors, no drop flaps and only one side door, located on the left.

B201589 (opposite top) is one of the few survivors to retain Diagram 1/107 bodywork. These were quite rare by this time, only the occasional one or two still to be seen around. Note also the original oil axleboxes.

B281209 (opposite centre) was originally a 24.5T Mineral wagon (see Vol. 2, section 5, pages 18/19). It has kept its original springs and thus its original number.

B290429 (opposite lower) is one of the vehicles given new springs. These were numbered between B290000 to B290485, although not all these were ever produced. All these rebuilds were being withdrawn from service at the end of the review period.

B201589(Taken at Swansea Docks 12/3/83)
A very interesting modification to an original Diagram 1/107 vehicle is seen here, but it is not known how common this was, or even if the other side was similarly modified. The condition of the paint on the new plate suggests that it was carried out in the late 1970s. (Ref: W12746/DL)

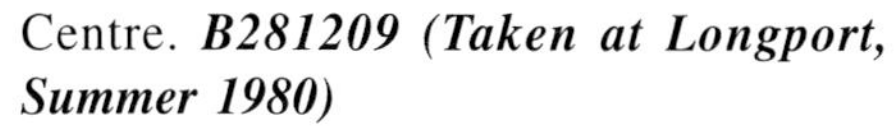

Centre. ***B281209 (Taken at Longport, Summer 1980)***
The mineral trains in the Stoke-on-Trent area showed a good mixture of types. This single door MDO is flanked by B316809 (opposite) and B200417 seen on page 5. Livery is Freight Brown with black underframe and white lettering. (Ref: W8078/DL)

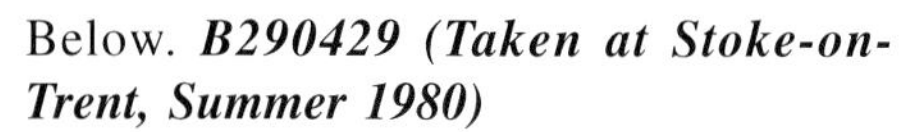

Below. ***B290429 (Taken at Stoke-on-Trent, Summer 1980)***
The single door MDO wagons that were rated at 25T were distinguishable only by the numbers. The axleboxes and buffers fitted depended what was on the host vehicle and there was no pattern. Although only about two years old, the paint is already peeling. Livery is as above. (Ref. W8097/DL)

Section 3. Iron Ore Tippler Wagons

B382974 (Taken at Middleton Towers, Summer 1980)
One of the few places where unfitted iron ore tippler wagons could still be found at the start of the review period was the Middleton Towers sand quarry near Kings Lynn, Norfolk. There were a number of other types to be found at this location (see sections 5 and 7) and I suspect the tipplers didn't travel very far. Livery is weathered grey with black underframe and white lettering on black panels. (Ref. W4846/DL)

The surviving traditional B.R. designs of the 1950s were beginning to fade away in the early 1980s. The iron ore tippler, in unfitted form, was only recorded in any numbers at Middleton Towers (see above). In a survey of wagon type totals conducted in 7/83, no MSOs were listed. However, the type lived on in civil engineer's use as ZKO spoil wagons.

Vacuum braked MSV wagons were slightly more numerous and in use on more than one traffic. B386313 (opposite upper) was also in the Middleton Towers sand traffic circuit and, as mentioned in the caption above, it is suspected that these only travelled a very short distance.

B385867 (opposite centre) is in use in a block train for stone traffic and is seen here heading empty back to Westbury. I can't quite recall the loaded destination but it could have been traffic to Angerstein Wharf for the construction of Thames Tidal Barrier.

In July 1983, there were still 1548 MSVs in traffic according to T.O.P.S., but these too would soon pass to the civil engineers as ZKV BARBEL wagons.

B384618 (opposite lower) represents the Ingot Mould version of the unfitted iron tippler. Many of these had part of the lower sides, outside of the vertical bracing, removed to allow workmen in the wagons to get out once the mould was loaded but this one lacks this modification. None of these wagons, which were coded SMO under T.O.P.S., were listed as in service in 7/83.

Opposite Centre. ***B385867 (Taken at Brixton, Summer 1980)***
The vacuum-braked iron ore tippler had been serving in stone traffic for a long time (see Vol. 1, page 27 for an early example). The B.R. policy was to use these vehicles either as an initial fleet for a traffic that would later have P.O. stock or for a short term flow such as the construction of the Thames Barrier at Charlton, Kent. Livery of this wagon is Freight Brown with black underframe and white lettering. (Ref: W8488/DL)

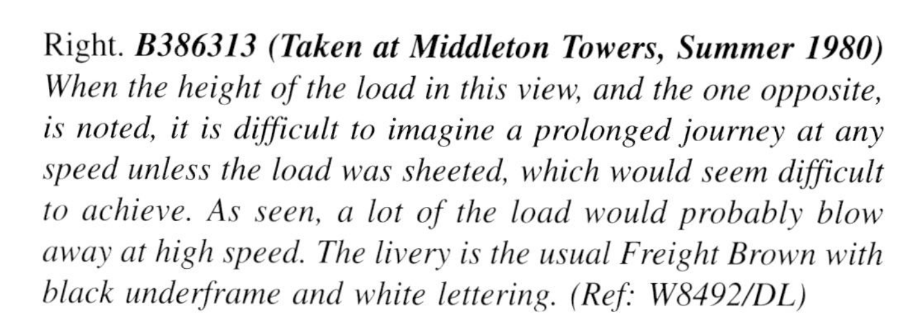

Right. ***B386313 (Taken at Middleton Towers, Summer 1980)*** *When the height of the load in this view, and the one opposite, is noted, it is difficult to imagine a prolonged journey at any speed unless the load was sheeted, which would seem difficult to achieve. As seen, a lot of the load would probably blow away at high speed. The livery is the usual Freight Brown with black underframe and white lettering. (Ref: W8492/DL)*

B384618 (Taken at Scunthorpe, Winter 1980)
The Ingot Mould wagons had a few more years service when this view was taken but, as mentioned in the text, all had gone by 1983. The cut out sides mentioned would have precluded their use as ZKO spoil wagons. A study of recorded examples, however, does suggest that not all were done. Livery is rust with yellow top edge and large panel (with black lettering) and white lettering on black panel.

Overall this picture provides an interesting contrast between the old and new orders of steel wagons. (Ref: W9699/DL)

Section 4. Highfit Wagons

B486872 (Taken at Tees Yard, Spring 1981)
The variations of the all-steel Highfits built after 1948 are rather numerous and hard to work out. The example shown here was built in 1952 to Diagram 1/041 with L.N.E.R. pattern bodywork, although with an unusual top capping and standard Morton pattern vacuum brakegear. There are similar vehicles on either side and the condition of them suggests recent use in lime traffic. Livery is Freight Brown with black underframe and white lettering. (Ref: W9297/DL)

The 10' 0" wheelbase 13T Highfit was another type that would finally dwindle away during the review period. Their numbers had already been steadily depleted from the late 1960s onwards by both scrapping and the transfer of many vehicles to the departmental fleets, leaving those that remained in revenue service on 'special' traffic.

All-steel vehicles were coded OHV under the T.O.P.S. system and one traffic that these appear to have been retained for was lime, as seen above. The example shown opposite, however, could possibly have been in general use.

Vehicles with wooden bodywork, including those which still had tarpaulin bars, were coded OWV. One traffic that these seem to have been used on was the transport of rock salt - the material spread on roads by gritting lorries during the winter. This, obviously, was rather a seasonal traffic and such wagons would spend a lot of the year stored out of use. However, neither of the examples shown opposite were in such use. Both of these seem to have been used on general traffic, although in both cases, it does appear to have been a one-off loading.

By 7/83, OHV numbers were down to 34 and OWV numbers to 32. All were soon to be scrapped because they had only been a temporary stopgap in civil engineers spoil traffic, as the wooden ones, especially, suffered a lot of body damage. However, see section 15 for an interesting survival of the all-steel type.

Above. ***B479422 (Taken at Stoke-on-Trent, Summer 1980)***
B.R. Diagram 1/041 vehicles were fitted with both types of brakegear, this one having the L.N.E.R. pattern (compare with the Diagram 1/037 vehicle in Vol. 2, page 42). The high vacuum pipe was difficult to couple to the next pipe and they were often replaced. Livery is rust with white lettering on a Freight Brown panel.
(Ref: W9272/DL)

Centre. ***B477743 (Taken at Hoo Junction, Spring 1981)***
The Sheerness Steel works used scrap metal as its raw material and, at the start of the review period, this was usually conveyed in MCV wagons. Much rarer was the use of OWVs, one of which is seen here as a runner wagon for an overhanging load. Woodwork is unpainted and underframe and ends are rusty. Lettering is white. (Ref: W9269/DL)

Right. ***B478763 (Taken at Hoo Junction, Spring 1980)***
Traditional containers had disappeared nearly ten years earlier. The ones seen here for break up had been left, probably in use as a static store, in a goods yard and had been cleared out. Livery is much as above but with a bit of Freight Brown paint on the sides. (Ref: W9271/DL)

Section 5. B.R. 25.5T Hoppers

B438775 (Taken at Middleton Towers, Summer 1980)
The 25.5T iron hopper fleet was rather complex in its variations. The one seen here (and B439758, opposite lower) was built as an unfitted vehicle and converted to vacuum braking for sand traffic in 1971. This example is in service from Middleton Towers and, unlike the iron ore tipplers seen in section 3, they probably had a long journey ahead. Livery is Freight Brown with black underframe and white lettering. The code is SAND VB. (Ref: W8624/DL)

The 25.5T iron ore hopper wagons had been designed in the mid-1950s and remained fairly numerous at the start of the review period. First featured in Vol. 2, section 11, we return for a final look at the type before withdrawal, for, by 7/83, there were no HJOs, 235 HJVs and 580 HKVs.

The HJV fleet comprised several different variants. One of these, as illustrated above, had been converted as late as 1971. These vehicles were on sand traffic and Nos. were; B438000/5/19/53/5/62/95, B438149/56/61/8, B438230/99, B438320/7/44/78, B438413/37/60/2/77/96, B438507/8/96, B438637/49/71/3, B438721/9/31/43/75/87/93/6, B438800/3/4/12/29/31/5/74/5, B438910/57/61/74/80/7/95, B439010/8/28/47, B439102/29/36/63/6/98, B439225/54/69/77, B439322/52/3/8/61/2/4, B439416/35/48/54/63/73/4.

B437573 (opposite upper) was one of a batch built in 1957/58 with vacuum brakes for iron ore traffic and rated at 33.5T, thus becoming T.O.P.S. code HKV. These vehicles were Diagram 1/167 and numbers were B437500 to B437899.

Despite all the conversions, unfitted examples of the 25.5T iron ore hopper could still be seen (as opposite centre).

Finally B439758 (opposite lower) is an example of an unrecorded batch of vehicles converted for limestone traffic, others being B439717/59/81. Judging by the livery, these vehicles were converted post-1964 and may have been intended to replace some of the Diagram 1/165 vehicles numbered B439500 to B439699 (see Vol. 2, page 31). These had been up-rated to 33.5T for iron ore traffic of which six were in limestone traffic.

Above. ***B437573 (Taken at Middleton Towers, Summer 1980)***
The Diagram 1/167 vehicles had originally been used on iron ore traffic but had been transferred to sand traffic, either because of steel works closure or replacement by modern P.O. tippler wagons (see section 26). Livery is Freight Brown with black underframe and white lettering. (Ref: W8607/DL)

Centre. ***B438044 (Taken at Stoke-on-Trent, Autumn 1980)***
One of the first to be built, this 25.5T iron hopper is in original condition. These unfitted vehicles were operating out of Oakamoor sand quarry. Livery is Grey with black underframe and white lettering on black panels. Apart from the speed restriction and pool number, it remains in 1960s livery. (Ref: W8620/DL)

Right. ***B439758 (Taken at Dewsnap Yard, Spring 1981)***
The B.R. office dealing with rolling stock matters was pretty good at recording conversions in the 1960s, provided that they were informed. This limestone hopper does not appear in any records but, as detailed in the text, was not a one-off. Livery is Freight Brown with black underframe and white lettering. The sheet is grey and, judging by this and the location, it was still in limestone traffic. (Ref: W9332/DL)

Section 6. B.R. PRESFLO Wagons

B888181 (Taken at Peterborough, Summer 1980)
Some Presflos when first built were used on salt traffic but eventually ended their lives in fly ash traffic in the Peterborough area. However, being vacuum braked, they would not have worked with the genuine fly ash wagons of the CSA class which were air braked only. Nevertheless, there were enough of these vehicles to form a block train or two on their own. Livery was still I.C.I. Blue-Green and the location of the two I.C.I. symbols was in the light areas on the upper sides. Underframe was black and lettering white. Most carried the CPV T.O.P.S. code but unusually, this example doesn't. (Ref: W8344/DL)

Another group of vehicles for early withdrawal in the review period were the B.R. Presflo wagons. There were, however, 786 CPVs still in service in 7/83 and also 8 CPWs with ferry fittings for the old Fullers Earth traffic dating back to the 1950s.

In Vol. 2, page 32, an example plated RUGBY CEMENT was illustrated. Another, B873800, (opposite centre) is shown here and it gives a good view of the top and the vacuum cylinders.

Even the A.P.C.M. Co., despite their large fleet of company owned modern vehicles, continued to use some, as indicated by B873042 (opposite lower).

An interesting group of vehicles, not covered in this series so far, were the salt Presflo wagons. The I.C.I. company adopted this wagon type for its salt traffic and initially, vehicles selected at random were used. The first was B888002 (opposite upper) and this differed from the others, in that despite the lettering, it did not revert to cement traffic. Later vehicles in the range B888181 to B888200 were specially allocated to salt traffic and carried the special livery, as B888181 (above).

Later, the others passed into slate powder traffic from Wadebridge, at least by 1970 and possibly earlier. Nos. B888003/17/22/5/38/51/84/91, B888111/8/21/8/9/48/50/5/60/2/3/4 were used initially in this traffic before they too reverted to cement traffic.

By the review period, however, all these vehicles were to be found in fly ash traffic in the Peterborough area.

B888002 (Taken at Peterborough, Summer 1980)
As well as the vehicles opposite, there were other salt carrying vehicles around and, as they had differences in loading and discharge, they too ended up in the fly ash fleet. As far as is known, B888002 is the only one to have shaker pockets, the features on the lower side. Livery is Freight Brown with black underframe and white lettering. (Ref: W8335A/DL)

B873800 (Taken at Tonbridge, Spring 1980)
Buffers and the position and number of the vacuum brake cylinders differed from batch to batch. B873800 is one of the later vehicles, built in 1964. Livery is Freight Brown under the usual cement dust with black underframe and white lettering. Nameplate is black on orange and a clean example will be found in Vol. 2, page 32. (Ref: W8328/DL)

B873042 (Taken at Hoo Junction, Summer 1980)
B873042 was built in 1960 but appears to have the same characteristics as the one above. Although the A.P.C.M. allocated vehicles had originally carried plates, (see Vol. 1, page 31), the few still used during the review period did not. Livery is as above but, instead of a plate, there was a yellow W. This indicated 'Walcrete', a brand of cement manufactured by A.P.C.M. (Ref: W8318/DL)

Section 7. B.R. Covhop Wagons

B886273 (Taken at Workington, 22/5/82)
The tripolyphosphate Covhop conversions appear to have been done quite early in their life but no record has been kept. From ground level, you had to get a long way back to see the four circular hatches which identified them. Livery is rusty with a good coat of grime, any lettering visible being white. (Ref: W11550/DL)

Some of the traditional Covhop fleet seemed to have had a brief flowering in a new life about this time but faded away during the review period.

By 7/83, there were no unfitted vehicles coded CCO for Rockware Glass traffic and only 18 CCVs. All the unfitted CHOs had also gone by then, leaving 149 CHPs and 53 CHVs, presumably in soda ash traffic.

The Covhop was featured in Vol. 1, page 35, and Vol. 2, page 37. In their lives, bodywork was generally unmodified, however, the vehicles for tripolyphosphate traffic, illustrated above, did get minor modifications. The large rectangular top hatches were fixed down and four small circular hatches were fitted along the centre line. Recorded examples appear within the ranges B886010 to B886081, B886272 to B886275, B886402 to B886407 and B886763 to B886778 but also noted outside these ranges were B870519 and B886974.

B886144 (opposite upper) and B870538 (opposite centre) represent examples of the fleet especially lettered for sand traffic from Middleton Towers to Rockware Glass Ltd. in the Doncaster area. I don't have a full list of numbers but have recorded all the following photographically; CCP (B870505/9/17/28/35/6/49/53/77, B870688, B870742, B886640/97, B886706/32). CCV (B870-813/28/54/9/65/9/70/2/4/6), CCO (B886007, B886144, B886292, B886355, B886447/57/75/98).

Another livery variant (opposite lower) was used for bulk urea traffic between Tees-side and Great Chesterford, near Cambridge. Examples of these were numbered B870698, B870702/8/42 and B886711/48.

Above. ***B886144 (Taken at Middleton Towers, Summer 1980)***
I have not been able to establish exactly when vehicles painted in ROCKWARE GLASS livery first appeared. However, as I have a photograph of one of the CCPs in 1969 with no such lettering, it was presumably after then. Unfitted vehicles do not appear to have been all that common. B886144 was in weathered Rail Grey with black underframe. All lettering is white on black.
(Ref: W8299/DL)

Centre. ***B870538 (Taken at Doncaster, Winter 1980)***
It is thought likely that these vacuum piped vehicles were withdrawn soon after the delivery of the vehicles covered in section 28 of this volume. Since this was one of the final uses of the class, withdrawal seems a likely outcome. Livery is dirty Freight Brown, other details being as above.
(Ref: W9750/DL)

Right. ***B870698 (Taken at Northwich, Summer 1980)***
The bulk urea Covhops worked from Billingham-on-Tees to a depot in Cambridgeshire and only vacuum piped wagons appear to have been used on this service. The vehicles on this traffic appear to have been replaced at the start of the review period but do not seem to have been scrapped immediately, rather, they returned to soda ash traffic as seen here. Livery is Freight Brown with black underframe and white lettering. (Ref: W8257/DL)

Section 8. 4 wheeled Steel Wagons (Traditional)

B730560 (Taken at Battersea, South Lambeth, Summer 1980)
As well as for steel traffic, tube wagons were often used for general loads too big to fit in a highfit. That is probably the reason for this one being in the environs of the old G.W.R. South Lambeth goods depot which, although closed, played host to an S&T depot involved with a re-signalling scheme. Livery is Freight Brown with black underframe and white lettering. (Ref: W8757/DL)

Traditional four wheeled steel carrying wagons were still to be found during the review period. There were 1432 STV Tube wagons and 674 SOV Pipe wagons, a fair number of each. SPV Plate wagons were reduced in number to 170. This was because of the fact that many had been converted to KEV, KRV and RRV configuration.

Most of the STV fleet came from the vacuum braked B.R. standard design, as shown above. These came within the number ranges B730500 to B730649, B730650 to B730999, B732040 to B733039, B733040 to B733219 and B733240 to B733459, there being considerable buffer and axlebox variety.

The only other type of tube wagon still to be seen was the ex-L.N.E.R. design to Diagram 1/445, as shown opposite upper. These were numbered B730000 to B730499.

SOV pipe wagons were within the ranges B484150 to B484199, B740000 to B740299, B740600 to B741729 (push brakes and various buffers), B740300 to B740599 (L.N.E. brakes and spindle buffers, see opposite centre), B741730 to B741749 (push brakes and Dowty buffers) and B741750 to B741949 (clasp brakes and OLEO buffers). Fifty of the last batch were converted to ODA by July 1983.

SPV plate wagons were in the B93xxxx range, most being the B.R. standard design but at least one (opposite lower) being of L.N.E. design.

Opposite Top. ***B730260 (Taken at Sheerness, Summer 1980)***
Vehicles with L.N.E. vacuum brakegear were all built in the early 1950s but, as this page shows, survived as long as the others. B730260 is a Diagram 1/445 wagon, and only the bearings have changed (to roller bearings) since it was built. Livery is weathered bauxite with black underframe and white lettering. (Ref: W8753/DL)

Opposite Centre. ***B740551 (Taken at Battersea, Longhedge Jct., Spring 1980)***
This view is doubly rare. The wagon itself is one of the few Diagram 1/461 vehicles not rebuilt as a container wagon in the 1950s. It was also very rare by this time to see a full train of these pipe wagons, possibly this was one of the last. Livery is weathered bauxite with black underframe and white lettering. (Ref: W8115/DL)

Right. ***B933259 (Taken at Stoke-on-Trent, Summer 1980)***
As with the Diagram 1/461 pipe wagons, the Diagram 1/432 plate wagons had also been subject to a conversion programme, this time to timber wagons. However, being more numerous, they were not quite so rare in original form, although this one has been fitted with HYBOX axleboxes. Loaded with Olive Green army trailers, livery is rusty with white lettering. (Ref: W10098/DL)

Section 9. Bogie Bolster C and D (VB types)

B927471 (Taken at Cargo Fleet, Autumn 1981)
In suitably appropriate surroundings, this view shows the dual nature of steel traffic at the start of the review period. Working from the back, the line in the rear are all air braked BDA wagons. Moving forward, the vehicles on the left and right are Diagram 1/478 BDV wagons. The main wagon, B927471 is a Diagram 1/484 BDV and the runner on the right is a cut-down Diagram 1/420 timber wagon. All the front row are rusty with white lettering. (Ref: W9125/DL)

The vacuum braked variants of the 30T Bogie Bolster C and 42T Bogie Bolster D remained prominent during the review period and there were two varieties of each type.

B922500 to B923099 and B945791 to B945990 were Diagram 1/477 BCV wagons with plate bogies and roller bearings (opposite lower).

B923100 to B923299 and B924400 to B924799 were also BCV wagons to Diagram 1/477 but these had Gloucester pattern bogies and roller bearings (opposite centre). This type was used for a number of conversions, such as BTV pipe wagons, and both these and the BCVs were given air through pipes to become BCW or BTW.

B927600 to B927799 were BDV wagons built to Diagram 1/478 and had plate bogies and roller bearings (opposite upper).

B927400 to B927599 and B927800 to B928199 were BDV wagons, to Diagram 1/484 in the case of the second batch, there not being a correct diagram for the first batch. Both these batches had Gloucester bogies and roller bearings (above). Quite a few vehicles from the second batch were converted to FEV container wagons and both these and those remaining as BDV were given air pipes to become BDW and FEW respectively.

Opposite Top. ***B927731 (Taken at Hoo Junction, Summer 1980)***
Seen here carrying the long beams from a 50T PARROT case wagon, B927731 is in original condition. These vehicles were restricted in speed because of the bogie type and were not considered for fitting with air pipes. The livery is rusty with white lettering. (Ref: W8797/DL)

Centre. ***B924439 (Taken at Tees Yard, Spr. 1981)*** *Some bogie bolster wagons were beginning to appear with the blue nylon straps that replaced chains on the BDA conversions (see opposite for the differences) and they were the ones that were also air piped. B924439 has the strap mountings but not the straps. Livery is faded bauxite and white lettering. (Ref: W8464/DL)*

Right. ***B945877 (Taken at Battersea, Stewarts Lane, Spring 1980)***
The BCV wagons with plate bogies suffered from the same speed restriction as the BDVs and were not thus eligible to receive air pipes. Neither type featured in conversions perhaps for this reason. Livery is rusty with white lettering. (Ref: W8104A/DL)

Section 10. Other Bogie Steel Wagons (Traditional)

B924429 (Taken at Toton Yard, Summer 1980)
The BOV bogie pipe wagons were a short lived attempt to provide bogie vehicles for the pipe traffic carried from the works at Stanton Gate, Derbyshire. The loads carried were similar to those on the BSCO wagons featured in section 25 of this volume but use seems to have been very brief. Livery was Freight Brown with black underframes and white lettering. (Ref: W8740/DL)

As mentioned in the previous section, the Diagram 1/477 Bogie Bolster C wagons with Gloucester bogies and roller bearings were used for conversions. One such was the BOV bogie pipe wagon, as shown above. These appear to have been converted circa 1974 and were numbered as follows: B924429/34/53/65/6/79/80/8/95/9, B924504/7/9/18/24/5/9/32/59/67/77/9/92/3/6, B924602/3/11/25/31/5/6/41/5/55/66/7/8/78/86/91/2, B924705/35/58/9/62/6/73/87/8/9/92. They were stored by 1980 and were soon broken up.

Bogie Bolster E wagons in original form (opposite upper) were comparatively few in number during the review period, there being 140 listed as in service in 7/83, from the original batch of 300 (see Vol. 2, page 66).

Borail wagons were never that numerous and unfitted examples, even in departmental use, were rare in the review period. DS64631 (opposite centre) was a particular rarity.

B.R. built Borail wagons came in three forms. The earliest were unfitted but, after a twilight existence, re-emerged as JXO coil wagons (see section 12). The most numerous were the fish-belly type of Diagrams 1/482 and 1/483. These, in most cases, were given air brakes as BRA and will be covered in the next volume in this series. This left the BRP vehicles of Diagram 1/481 (opposite lower) which were numbered B946050 to B946064. All had gone by 7/83.

Opposite top. ***B923879 (Taken at Stoke-on-Trent, Summer 1980)***
The BEV was rather too short for the steel traffic of the 1980s. This example is, in fact, acting as a runner wagon to another BEV, B924152, which appears to be carrying rail. Livery is dirty bauxite with black underframe and white lettering. The reason for the number being painted on the centre side is not known. (Ref: W5231/DL)

Opposite Centre. ***DS64631 (Taken at Doncaster, Winter 1980)***
Wagons that could carry 60' 0" lengths of rail, which had become the standard before the introduction of continuously welded rail, were jealously guarded by each region. When the S.R. went fully fitted, they no longer needed unfitted stock and these passed to the E.R. DS64631 was always a civil engineers vehicle but was identical to traffic wagons to S.R. Diagram 1598. Livery is rusty with white lettering. (Ref: W9199/DL)

Opposite Lower. ***B946054 (Taken at Queenborough, Spr. 1980)***
As mentioned above, the 60' 0" rails were replaced by c.w.r. This meant that there was a need to convey old rail to be scrapped. By the review period, this was often done by a shorter wagon using runners. When available, the proper wagons could be used, as seen here. Livery is weathered bauxite with rusty bogies and white lettering. The BRP code is carried and is just behind the first stanchion. (Ref: W9191/DL)

B924152

B946054

Section 11. Boplate Wagons and Variations

B947910 (Taken at Wakefield, Summer 1980)
To replace four wheeled coke wagons, which were of an elderly design and largely unfitted, vacuum braked boplate wagons were converted to carry two large containers of coke from Wakefield to Derwenthaugh, on Tyneside. There were generally few differences amongst the wagons, but the container designs did differ slightly. These were dirty grey with white lettering and the container flats were usually just rusty with any surviving lettering in white. (Ref: W9166/DL)

Unfitted boplate wagons coded BPO (opposite centre) were getting rare at the start of the review period. By 7/83, 80 had been converted to BPA (see section 22 of this volume) and the remainder scrapped. Of the vacuum braked variants, only 87 of both were in use. However, many of these had been converted to other types as detailed below.

One traffic using BPV conversions was the coke container traffic from Wakefield to Newcastle.

As with the BCV and BDV wagons covered in section 9, there were two bogie variations. B947860 to B948009 had Gloucester bogies and roller bearings and B948010 to B948409 had plate bogies and roller bearings. From the first batch (see above) the following were converted to FEV coke container wagons: B947883/7/91/6, B947905/10/9/20/3/8/30/43/58/64/6/92. These were eligible for air pipes and all were fitted by 7/83.

From the second batch (opposite upper), the following were converted: B948045/85/97, B948130/98, B948200/12/27/52/3/68, B948358/62, B928405. These remained FEV and all variants were out of service by 1987.

The following vehicles had been converted from the first batch to Boflat/FWV wagons (opposite lower), which could carry either steel coil or vehicles. These were numbered B947863/4/5/6/7/9/70/2/3/4/5/7/8/81/2/4/5/6/8/9/92/4/5/7/8/9, B947900/1/2/3/4/7/8/9/11/4/5/8/22/4/5/6/7/9/31/2/4/5/8/9/40/1/2/4/5/7/8/9/51/3/4/5/6/7/9/61/2/3/5/7/8/71/2/4/6/8/9/80/1/2/4/6/7/8/9/90/1/4/5/6/7/9, B948004/6/8/9. These were eligible for air pipes and a few were fitted. The type was not used much and was broken up by the end of the review period.

Opposite centre. ***B947464 (Taken at Scunthorpe, Summer 1980)***
Scunthorpe was a traditional area for boplate wagons, as the steel works produced large plate for shipbuilding, etc. It is therefore an appropriate place to photograph one of the last unfitted BPO wagons recorded by myself. Livery is original grey and the chassis is rusty. The white lettering on black panel is original and there is no sign of a T.O.P.S. code.
(Ref: W8891/DL)

Right. ***B948405 (Taken at Wakefield, Summer 1980)***
Without the containers, the FEV was merely a bogie wagon chassis. Some, like the vehicle here, retained the plate ends, but this was not common. Livery is rusty with white lettering. (Ref: W9180/DL)

B947932 (Taken at Hoo Junction, Spring 1981)
The FWV Boflat conversion was rather elusive and I only found a few under load with steel coil. This high angle view shows the new floor and guard rails and also the new drop ends. Livery was Freight Brown with black underframe and white lettering. Note the typical repair siding features; compressed air cylinder and pipes for air powered tools. (Ref: W9188B/DL)

Section 12. Strip Coil Wagons

B923386 (Taken at Longport, Summer 1980)
The JPV class were conversions from Bogie Bolster E wagons (see section 10 of this volume) and there were quite a few variations in how the load was carried. With this example, two of the bolsters were fixed lengthwise and the coils positioned over the bogie in the usual way. Another JPV in the same train had lost the bolsters altogether and the single coil was mounted on cradles in the centre of the wagon. Livery is rusty with white lettering. Sheeting is blue plastic. (Ref: W8922/DL)

Strip coil was not a load carried much by rail until steel works began to close in the 1960s and many of the types subsequently allocated to it were converted from other vehicle types. Many of these could still be seen at the start of the review period and the examples in this section formed part of one strip coil train.

The JPV class (above) was a fairly late conversion in 1975 to replace four wheeled ex-Palbrick wagons which themselves had only been converted in 1970. The source vehicle was the short Bogie Bolster E and numbers were as follows: B923345/67/85/6, B923420/1/45/7/50/5/83, B923526/9/54/6, B923602/6/7/13/8/35/42/68/89/90, B923714/5/34/58/78, B923824/44/54/9/78/90/5/6, B923906/9/17/28/56/68/76/91/2, B924042/9/75, B924107/9/27/49/51/3, B924220/44/9/53/65/83/4, B924318/23/34/53/9/60/89, B924813/21/36/73.

As mentioned in the caption above, there were variations in the way the coils were positioned and carried.

The JMV class (opposite upper) were Bogie Bolster Ds without the bolster stanchions and two coils positioned over the bogies. These had originally operated from the Corby steelworks and carried the legend CORBY COIL. Numbers were as follows: B927428/43/61/3/75/6/8/83/5, B927538/73/84/6/94, B927622/44/78/80/5/96, B927751/8/63/88/93/4/6, B927801/17/30/81, B927909/12/53/71/83, B928004/14/38/55/65, B928101/18/20/44/6/71/3/96.

The JXO class (opposite centre) were formerly unfitted Borail wagons and thus 60' 0" long. These were refurbished in 1975 and renumbered B960000 to B960023.

Finally, the KGO class (opposite bottom) were converted, possibly around 1975, from Hot Pig Iron wagons. Numbers were as follows: B744629/30/40/5/8/52/7/60/3/4/6/8/74/5/7/82/5/90/1/5, B744701/2/9/10/3/7/9/35/6/7/8/9/42/5/55.

Above. ***B927796 (Taken at Longport, Summer 1980)***
There was no attempt to select a particular BDV variant when converting them to CORBY COIL wagons in the 1960s. The example shown here has plate bogies (see section 9 of this volume for BDV numbers and bogie details). Livery is rusty with white lettering and blue plastic sheeting. (Ref: W8920/DL)

Centre. ***B960005 (Taken at Longport, Summer 1980)***
The JXO class are something of a mystery type. Built in 1949 as BORAIL WE wagons numbered B946000 to B946049, it would have been expected that they would have turned up in the civil engineers fleet. Instead, 24 became JXO and at least one other remained in general traffic afterwards. Livery is as above. (Ref: W8914/DL)

Right. ***B744677 (Taken at Longport, Summer 1980)***
The Hot Pig Iron wagons were rather a specialised type but could still be seen in original form in the early 1970s. Most were then scrapped but 35 had the central end section lowered to allow coils to be loaded. They were normally sheeted when loaded, as here, livery being as above. Both this class and the JXO above were soon withdrawn but 23 JMVs and 16 JPVs remained in service in 7/83. (Ref: W8917/DL)

Section 13. Lowmac and Rectank Wagons

B909031 (Taken at Tees Yard, Spring 1981)
The B.R. Rectank wagon was a straight development of a design built during World War 1 to carry the first tanks, hence the code name. Being so low, they were only vacuum through piped because there was no place to put a vacuum cylinder without it fouling the track. Despite the XRP T.O.P.S. code, this example looks to be in use as a runner wagon and should be an RRP. Livery is rusty with weathered wooden floor and white lettering. (Ref: W9922/DL)

Traditional wagons to carry motor vehicles were not in great demand for their original traffic during the review period. The biggest user, the Ministry of Defence, now had a fleet of refurbished Warwell wagons to carry the loads previously handled by the Lowmac and Rectank fleet. They were not immediately withdrawn, however, many being used as runner wagons.

The Rectank fleet (above) had only been built in 1960 (details of numbers being found in Vol. 1, page 74) and were of less use because they were only vacuum through piped. None were in service as either XRP or RRP in 7/83. They were not used for civil engineers plant and it is probable that they were scrapped.

The Lowmac fleet was far more varied and the vacuum braked survivors remained in service

B904112 (opposite upper) and B904117 (opposite centre) were both built in 1955 to Lot 2592. The diagram was 2/245 and the numbers were B904105 to B904119. They were originally allocated to the Eastern and North Eastern Regions and coded LOWMAC ET. A version was also built with roller bearings.

B904511 (opposite lower) was built in 1951/52 to Lot 2187. Diagram was 2/242 and the numbers were B904500 to B904537. They were also allocated to the Eastern and North Eastern Regions and were coded LOWMAC EP. Once again, there was a roller bearing version of the type.

As RRV wagons, they probably lasted to the end of the review period. Some may then have passed to the civil engineers but not many, as Flatrol wagons were preferred.

Right. ***B904112 (Taken at Portsmouth, Winter 1980)***
One of the last genuine vehicle traffics to be handled by Lowmacs were new ambulances from Wadham Stringer Ltd. The one seen here is for use in Scotland. This design of Lowmac originated with the G.W.R. but became one of the B.R. standard types. Livery is rusty with white lettering. The ambulance is white with blue stripe. (Ref: W10047/DL)

Centre. ***B904117 (Taken at Middlesborough, Spring 1980)***
Built to the same batch as the vehicle above, this wagon is in runner use and is seen here with other RRV wagons converted from SPV plate wagons. The design was rated at 20T and none of the G.W.R. vehicles were vacuum braked. Note that the vacuum pipe appears on one side of the wagon only. Livery is rusty with white lettering. (Ref: W10048/DL)

Below. ***B904511 (Taken at Portsmouth, Winter 1980)***
Despite also being coded as a runner, this Lowmac was recorded at Portsmouth and may also have been there for loading with an ambulance. This type was rated at 25T and had been a joint L.M.S./L.N.E.R. design which also became a B.R. standard. As with all the others, livery is rusty with white lettering. (Ref: W10056/DL)

Section 14. Brake Vans

B950653 (Taken at Leyton P.W. Depot, Stratford, East London, Spring 1980)
Although technically still in general traffic use, the location of this view suggests that B950653 should have been in civil engineers use. Flanked by an LMS D1657 vacuum piped brake van (built c. 1930 and a very rare survivor) and a World War II unfitted S.R. brake van, B950653 was supposedly to the standard Diagram 1/504. The very early built vehicles, as this one, had more lamp brackets and a tall vacuum pipe, as seen here. (Ref: W9204/DL)

Brake vans were still to be seen at the start of the review period but their numbers in revenue earning general traffic were becoming limited. Most were vacuum through piped but this detail was, in fact, rather irrelevant because they were used only on unfitted trains.

Almost all the types still in use were to the two B.R. standard diagrams. Diagram 1/504 vehicles had been built with vacuum through pipes and were numbered B950616 to B950865, B9511116 to B951275, B951516 to B951715, B952006 to B952165 and B952716 to B954520. The way to identify these from L.N.E.R. built vehicles when the number is not visible is by the foot boards, which ran full length, and by the end platforms, which were fitted with a concrete weight. B950653 (above) was an early vehicle and has non-standard lamp brackets and vacuum pipe.

In early B.R. days, some vehicles were built unfitted and were given Diagram 1/506. These were numbered B950866 to B951115, B951276 to B951515, B951716 to B952005 and B952166 to B952715. Quite a large number of these were later vacuum piped and these can be identified by a white pipe recessed into one side. B951109 (opposite upper) shows a van with one of about four variants of this feature.

The final batch of brake vans built, to Diagram 1/507, had vacuum through pipes, roller bearings and OLEO buffers. These were numbered B954521 to B955247 and most were fitted with air through pipes from the mid-1960s (as opposite centre).

Finally, for comparison, an original L.N.E.R. Diagram 61 brake van, the first version of this design is represented by a vehicle in engineers use (opposite lower).

B951109 (Taken at Worksop, Winter 1980)
This is another early Diagram 1/504 brake van and has the extra lamp bracket on the end. As it was unfitted when built, it does not have a high vacuum pipe. The side pipe was for the guard's release valve and couldn't come up through the floor as the chassis was filled with scrap for weight purposes. Livery is faded Bauxite with black underframe and white lettering on black panels. (Ref: W9210/DL)

B954816 (Taken at Tees Yard, Spring 1981)
The Diagram 1/507 brake vans fitted with air pipes were converted for use with HAA trains. With the abolition of brake vans on all fitted freights, they were used only where trains carried dangerous goods or where there was a special need for a guard such as with propelling manoeuvres. This example is Freight Brown with yellow stripes, black underframe and white lettering.(Ref: W9228/DL)

DE187699 (Taken at Portsmouth, Spr. 1980)
The L.N.E.R. had developed the design which became the B.R. standard for its Green Arrow express freight in the 1930s and the van seen here is a late survivor of the first design. The various lamp brackets were used to denote to other trains which line the train was travelling on. Now in departmental use, livery is faded Olive Green with black underframe and white lettering. (Ref: W9249/DL)

Section 15. Early Air Braked Wagons

TDC920500 (Taken at Tiverton Junction, 19/3/83)
During the review period, I spent a lot of time at the B.R. Rolling Stock Library researching wagon history and, on Fridays, was able to look on the T.O.P.S. computer for the location of rare stock. This led me to Tiverton for the prototype SAA and I also found other interesting types shown on succeeding pages in this volume. TDC920500 was in dirty Freight Brown livery with unpainted wooden partitions. Underworks were black and lettering was white. (Ref: W5682/DL)

The SAA type, featured in Vol. 2, page 83, was preceded by a prototype, 920500 (above), built in 1966. This vehicle was found in use as an oil train barrier wagon in 1983 but it is not known when the vertical partitions seen were fitted or what their function was intended to be.

Mention was made in Vol. 2, page 82 of air braked highfits. One of these is shown opposite upper.

These vehicles operated in a WR test train with Vans and Palvans. The vans were numbered B778246, B778331, B780046, B780465, B780575, B781007, B781263, B781375, B781479, B781595, B786001 and B786393, the penultimate being illustrated opposite centre.

The Palvans were numbered B778971, B779026, B779834, B781763, B781847, B781864 and B781875.

For the record, the other vehicles used in the test train were Tube wagons B730595, B731597, B732039 and B733045 and Plate wagons B934398, B935416, B935653, B935793 and B936129.

All these vehicles, after their testing finished, passed into general traffic. By the review period, the highfits, vans and Palvans were all in departmental use but were regularly seen on SPEEDLINK services. The Tubes had been barrier wagons at the start of the review period, but were not to be seen anywhere, whilst some of the Plates were seen carrying coal containers in Scotland. This latter traffic will be covered in Volume 4.

ADB476472 (Taken at Hoo Junction, Summer 1980)

All the highfits converted for the W.R. test train were all-steel with the L.N.E.R. pattern vacuum brake but it is not known whether this was deliberate policy or mere chance. Livery is Olive Green with black underworks and white lettering. T.O.P.S. code is ZGB. (Ref: W9261A/DL)

ADB786001 (Taken at Dover, Spring 1981)

The highfits and vans were to be seen anywhere in the country delivering spare parts to wagon repair sidings. That is the reason ADB786001 is seen at Dover between two ferry vans. Note the very complex new brakegear. Livery is as above and T.O.P.S. code is ZRB. (Ref: W6645/DL)

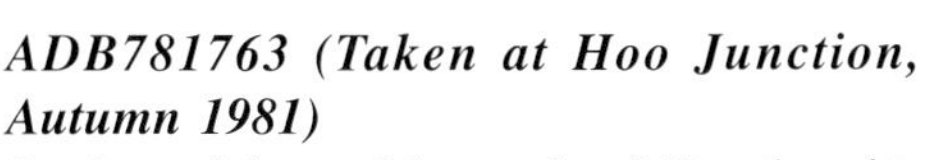

ADB781763 (Taken at Hoo Junction, Autumn 1981)

In view of the problems of stability that this type had in the 1960s, they were an unusual choice for air braking. The new pipes are well illustrated in this view. Livery is again Olive Green with black underworks and white lettering. Although different to ADB786001 above, the T.O.P.S. code was again ZRB. (Ref: W9759/DL)

Section 16. Air Braked Open Wagons

112024 (Taken at Rochester, 14/3/82)
This useful high-angle view of part of Rochester freight terminal reveals only air braked stock with a new OCA in the foreground. This class was a straight development of the SPA Plate wagon and had three part dropsides. The fitting of raised ends, introduced in the OBA seen beyond 112024, was not continued. Livery is Flame Red with black underworks and white lettering.
(Ref: W10419/DL)

The OAA class, seen opposite upper and covered in Vol. 2, page 82, were provided with their own large plastic sheets. The example shown opposite, however, does not have a sheet of that type, rather it appears to have two shorter ones overlapped. The traffic shown here was believed to be rolls of paper for newsprint.

The OBA was also covered in Vol. 2 page 83 and the class began to be fitted with Bruninghaus springs during the review period. The wagon shown opposite centre still has the original springs but is one of two recorded with the experimental Flame Red/White livery, the other being vehicle number 110051.

A new open wagon design, the OCA, appeared during the review period. Nos. 112000 to 112399 were built in 1981/82 and were the last air braked opens constructed to a new design. As will be seen in Volume 4 of this series, such vehicles were no longer required for general traffic by the end of the decade.

The final class available for air braked duties was somewhat older, and had replaced the ferry highbar wagons (see Vol. 2, Page 82) on continental duties. This was a version of the standard B.R. 22T tube wagon built in 1961 and it is illustrated opposite lower. Numbered GB733220 to GB733239 during the review period, they were still in Continental use and carried U.I.C. numbers. T.O.P.S. code was IOX.

Right. ***100008 (Taken at Battersea, Longhedge Junction, Spring 1980)***
Seven years after the introduction of T.O.P.S. it was still possible to find vehicles with old codes. This OAA still carries the code OPEN AB. Still in original Freight Brown livery, it also had the old double arrow and ABN symbols, the latter seen in Vol. 2, page 82. The sheet is semi-opaque blue plastic. (Ref: W8997/DL)

Centre right. ***110044 (Taken at Rochester, Spring 1981)***
Before settling on Flame Red and Freight Grey as the new RAILFREIGHT livery to replace maroon, certain vehicles were tried out in other colours. This OBA has Flame Red upper sides and ends, white lower sides, black underworks and white lettering, some on a black panel. (Ref: W9040A/DL)

Below. ***21 70 609 4 041-8 (Taken at Brixton, Summer 1980)***
GB733221, carrying the U.I.C. number when photographed, is loaded with a pair of wagon wheels and may be destined for Europe to aid a defective British owned wagon! There was little genuine export traffic for these wagons and they would soon become service vehicles performing the same duties. Livery was bauxite with black underframe. (Ref: W8768/DL)

Section 17. Air Braked Vans (VDA)

201047 (Taken at St. Blazey, Summer 1981)
The earlier air braked variant vans were somewhat difficult to tell apart because, although they had different door handle arrangements, the ends were all similar. The VDA class however, had a very distinctive end with external bracing. Livery is maroon with black underworks and white lettering. (Ref: W9021/DL)

After experimenting with various door patterns, B.R. settled on the VDA as what could be regarded as the 'standard' air braked van. First appearing during the previous review period (see Vol. 2, page 7), they became the ubiquitous air braked van of the 1980s.

Nos. 200650 to 200979 were built in 1976 and 210100 to 210399 in 1977/78. This was the most common variant, as illustrated by 200745 (opposite centre).

200980 to 200999 were given a different design code, presumably on account of the clasp brakegear, just visible. All appear, however, to have been allocated to the Rowntrees chocolate traffic which could explain the difference. 200987 (opposite lower) is an example of this batch, which was built in 1976.

Nos. 201000 to 201099 were certainly different because they had Taperlite suspension. This variant, illustrated above, was built in 1975/76.

The reason that no vehicles numbered 201100 to 210099 have appeared was due to a slip of the pen. The person issuing numbers, when doing the next batch after the Taperlite vans got the second and third digits swapped and the error was realised to late for it to be changed!

Opposite Lower. ***200987 (Taken at Dover, Spring 1981)***
The twenty vans of Lot 3890, 200980 to 200999, all seem to have been allocated to chocolate traffic and they may have had internal modifications. One however, 200987, was painted in a white livery overall, except for the underworks, which were black. The reason for this livery is unknown, although it may be for similar reasons as outlined in the caption for 200745. It appears to have carried this livery until it was withdrawn prior to 1991. There was no symbol or fleetname but the other lettering was black. (Ref: W9018/DL)

200934(Taken at Peterborough 10/10/82)
The Flame Red/Rail Grey livery was introduced for vans and some open wagons during the review period and was quite eye catching when new. This freshly re-painted vehicle clearly shows the division of colours. It soon weathered (see 230339, page 9) and within five years yet another livery was introduced. Note also the difference in end ribbing. (Ref: W12305/DL)

Centre. ***200745 (Taken at Dover, Spring 1981)***
VDA vans were the only class allocated to chocolate traffic from Rowntree, York and they had very easily identifiable white roofs. It is believed that this was used to minimise heat absorption from the sun, similar in principle to insulated or refrigerated vehicles which are also often white. Otherwise this example is in standard maroon livery with black underworks and white lettering. (Ref: W9014/DL)

Section 18. Other Air Braked Vans

210400 (Taken at Rochester, Winter 1981)
Built in October 1981 and seen here soon after, the prototype VGA van was in the traditional goods yard at Rochester, possibly used as a demonstrator. Unlike earlier long wheelbase four wheeled vans, it did not follow the family pattern set up by the COV AB (see opposite and Vol. 2, page 81). It was almost identical to current European practise instead. Livery was silver with Flame Red ends and black underworks. The symbol and fleet name, which were transfers on the prototype only, were Flame Red and white. (Ref: W9029/DL)

A new class, the VGA (above), appeared during the review period and was a complete change of design. It featured all metal construction with sliding sides for easy access and a greater capacity to compete with the ever larger payload of road vehicles that were appearing at the time.

That apart, the VDA vans dealt with in the previous section were still the most numerous at this time, but the earlier designs were also to be seen throughout the system.

At this stage, no attempt had been made to remove vacuum through pipes from the older vehicles and 200003 (opposite lower) shows an original COV AB still carrying this feature. Photographed at Hoo Junction marshalling yard, it is seen with traditional stock, although it needs to be said that the container was there for scrapping and had been dumped in some forgotten location for at least ten years!

The older vans were still being refurbished and two freshly painted vehicles are seen here. 200250 (opposite upper) was built in 1970/71 and the batch was numbered 200250 to 200324. It, too, had vacuum through pipes, as seen here, and was coded VBB under T.O.P.S.

The VCA class was mentioned in Vol. 2 page 80, and 200377 (opposite centre) is another example of a class which was beginning to congregate in South Wales on steel traffic.

200250 (Taken at Brixton, Spring 1980)
Heading towards Dover on a ferry service, as witnessed by the German open wagon in front of it, 200250 represents the last batch of vans to have through vacuum pipes. This feature would soon be dropped, as would the traditional oil tail lamp. Livery is maroon with black underworks and white lettering. (Ref: W8999/DL)

200337 (Taken at Brixton, Winter 1980)
As they weathered, vans in maroon livery took on the hue of the previous Freight Brown. Only when fresh, as here, was the difference marked, the van on the left being Freight Brown. Note also that the location of the number box depended on the door handle location. Livery is as above. (Ref: W9007/DL)

200003 (Taken at Hoo Junction, Spring 1980)
Perhaps for the reason mentioned in the previous caption, the maroon livery was fairly quickly dropped for the Flame Red/ Grey livery. Thus many of the COV AB vans, as here, never appeared in maroon, but kept the old Freight Brown livery with black underworks and white lettering. (Ref: W8992/DL)

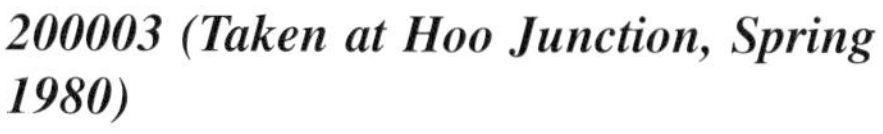

Section 19. B. R. Ferry Vans

21 70 219 9 028-8 (Taken at Battersea, Factory Junction, Spring 1980)
The ferry version of the B.R. CCT four wheeled parcels van was somewhat shorter and had no side windows. Curiously, close study of the photograph above appears to reveal window apertures, two on each side of the doors and one in the left hand door, that have been sheeted over. Livery was Freight Brown with black ends and underworks and with white lettering. (Ref: W8029/DL)

To supplement the fleet of air braked vans, B.R. had its fleet of ferry vans dating from the late 1950s and early 1960s.

The oldest vehicles were the 14T Ferry CCT vans built in 1958 and originally numbered GB889000 to GB889029. These were chiefly used in transporting motor vehicles to and from the continent but they were available for use in Britain and could run in SPEEDLINK trains. During the review period, they were phased out of use and some became barrier vans coded RBX under T.O.P.S. This type is illustrated above.

The B.R. ferry van was produced in some numbers in 1962/63 and had much in common with the long wheelbase pallet vans produced about the same time (see Vol. 2, page 49). Originally numbered GB786873 to GB787022 and GB787098 to GB787347, they resembled European stock closely but had very long sliding doors, an unusual feature for that late date. They could be seen in all parts of the system and 21 70 239 0 030-1 (opposite centre) shows a recently refurbished example.

As ferry vans, they were coded VIX but they were soon phased out of service in European traffic. For a time, they were reallocated to British use and were renumbered back into the normal series. They were given the code VJX but this use was very short lived and they reverted to RBX barrier wagons and other uses which will be dealt with in Volume 4 of this series.

A small number were converted to carry car parts, as seen opposite top (compare this with the Ford vehicles in Vol. 2, page 49). This use was not lengthy and, by the time of the photograph, they were stored out of use.

Right. ***21 70 219 6 020-8 (Taken at Peterborough, 10/10/82)***
This variant, of which there were 28 numbered 21 70 219 6 000-0 to 21 70 219 6 027-3, was used for carrying car components. Livery was light blue with black underparts and white lettering. (Ref: W12298/DL)

Centre. ***21 70 239 0 030-1 (Taken at Battersea, Factory Junction, Spring 1980)***
The B.R. ferry van fleet was spruced up at the start of the review period and many vehicles were given a new livery with latest symbols including the legend 'THROUGH TO THE CONTINENT BY BRITISH RAIL'. For whatever reason, probably the availability of stock with more modern running gear, their use on this traffic was short-lived. Livery is Flame Red upper body with Rail Grey lower parts, black chassis and white lettering. (Ref: W8026/DL)

Below. ***B787124 (Taken at Hoo Junction, 13/11/82)***
The ferry vans soon became restricted for use only in Britain and the proud boast was crudely painted over, as was the twelve digit U.I.C. number. Use as a VJX van is actually unlikely and most would probably have been barrier vans long before the recoding to RBX. Livery is as above with Freight Brown being used to paint out the letters and numbers. (Ref: W12426/DL)

Section 20. Air Braked Bogie Bolster (BDA)

950000 (Taken at Scunthorpe, Gunness Sdg., Winter 1980)
The prototype BDA was converted in 1975 from B942052, in company with two unfitted Bogie Bolster C wagons. These last remained as prototypes but the BDA became the most numerous air braked bogie bolster. 950000 eventually became ADC950000, a YNA GOLDFISH, with the C.M. and E.E. Livery is Freight Brown with black bogies and white lettering. (Ref: W9097/DL)

Having designed new air braked bogie bolsters (see sections 21 and 22), B.R. turned to refurbishment of existing unfitted stock for all other steel carrying bogie vehicles.

The 30T Bogie Bolster C was tried out in prototype form but it was only the 42T Bogie Bolster D which was produced in any numbers. The prototype, 950000 (above), was built in 1975 and was followed by a production batch 950001 to 950800 from 1977 to 1979. These vehicles could be identified by the lever brakes as shown by 950018 (opposite upper).

Two wagons, 950564 and 950565, have been recorded with a different pattern of bogie as 950565 (opposite centre) illustrates.

Further batches were built between 1979 and 1981, numbered 950801 to 951250, and these can be identified by the fitting of hand wheel hand brakes to the bogies and the abolition of the lever. 950811 (opposite lower) illustrates these later vehicles.

In due course, most of the early vehicles were transferred to the C.C.E. as YAA BRILL wagons but the type remained prominent in steel carrying duties for many years.

Opposite Top. ***950018 (Taken at Scunthorpe, Summer 1980)***
In steel producing areas, it was common to see a mixture of traditional stock and modern air braked stock. 950018, seen here, is marshalled between an unfitted BDO and an air braked XVA. Apart from the running gear, the BDA class was also fitted with blue nylon straps for securing the load instead of chains. Livery is Flame Red with black underworks and white lettering. (Ref: W8842/DL)

Opposite Centre. ***950565 (Taken at Scunthorpe, Gunness Sdg., Winter 1980)***
The vagaries of T.O.P.S. coding and the design codes issued are illustrated here. The T.O.P.S. Design code for 950000 (opposite) was BD006B but there appears to be no difference between it and 950018 (above), which was BD006C. 950565, shown here, plainly has different bogies but was still a BD006C. One can only assume that this experiment was not properly recorded in B.R. headquarters. Livery is Freight Brown with black bogies and white lettering. (Ref: W9105/DL)

950811 (Taken at Rochester, Spring 1981)
The load of 'H' girders on this later variant BDA is impressive and requires two SAA runners. The overhang to the left is extra long, however. Note the goods shed in the background, a traditional one which has lost its roof. The one at Scunthorpe (above) has at least retained this. Such locations were becoming increasingly rare. Livery of 950811 is Flame Red with black underworks and white lettering. (Ref: W9111/DL)

Section 21. Bogie Steel AB (BAA etc.)

900002 (Taken at Tees Yard, Spring 1981
The Bogie Steel AB was among the first of the new air braked designs to be built and, by the time of the review period, it was unusual to see one that had not been modified in one way or another. This was the third vehicle built and, as far as is known, is still in original condition. It retains vacuum through pipes, thus T.O.P.S. code is BAB. Livery is the original Freight Brown with black bogies and white lettering. (Ref: W9075/DL)

As noted above, the Bogie Steel AB was one of the earliest of the new air braked designs to appear. Although not delivered with prefixed numbers, they were delivered prior to the introduction of T.O.P.S. codes.

The first batch, 900000 to 900048, were air braked and vacuum through piped and were delivered in 1972. These, unmodified, were coded BAB under T.O.P.S. (as above). The rest 900049 to 900305 (excluding 900199, which was built as the prototype BBA, see section 22), were air braked only and coded BAA under T.O.P.S. when unmodified.

Quite early in their career, certain vehicles were converted, either temporarily or on a more permanent basis, to carry coils.

900236 (opposite upper) is fitted with five coil cradles and also has modified ends. It carries the incorrect T.O.P.S. BKA, which applies to the type illustrated at the bottom of this page, and this may mean that it once had longitudinal cradles.

900103 (opposite centre) has similar cradles to the vehicle above, but only four of them. It is coded BAA, indicating that the cradles were deemed by B.R. authorities as part of the load rather than a permanent fixture.

900013 (opposite lower) is fitted with a permanent longitudinal cradle made from two beams. These were known as 'kinky beams', hence the BKB/BKA classification under T.O.P.S. Vehicles known to have been so fitted were numbered as follows:

BKB (900001/6/9/12/3/4/9) BKA (900056/7/8/9/60/1/2/3/5/6/7/8/77/80/90/6/7), 900107/8/9/10/1/2/3/4/6/7/8/9/20/1/2/3/4/50/5/72/93/7, 900203/13/9/23/6/8/41/2/5/69/83/90/5, 900303.

Above. ***900236 (Taken at Tees Yard, Spring 1981)***
This vehicle at one stage operated as a BKA (see bottom plate) and is still carrying the painted T.O.P.S. code. This was presumably when the ends were modified, to allow for easier unloading. The five cradles seen fitted here are red and the wagon livery is Freight Brown with black bogies and white lettering. (Ref: W9087B/DL)

Centre. ***900103 (Taken at Tees Yard, Spring 1981)***
This wagon carries just four cradles and is otherwise unmodified. The load carried would normally be sheeted, as in the plate below, and was rolled sheet steel rather than coiled wire. This vehicle has been repainted with Flame Red ends, black underworks and white lettering. The cradles are again red. (Ref: W9079/DL)

Right. ***900013 (Taken at Tees Yard, Spring 1981)***
One of the vacuum through piped batch, this latter feature is hard to see tucked away below the left hand buffer. Note the unmodified ends, unlike the vehicle on the right, which has a different end modification to 900236, above. Livery is Freight Brown with black bogies and white lettering. The load is covered with a blue plastic sheet. (Ref: W9076/DL)

Section 22. Air Braked Steel Wagons (Other)

910460 (Taken at Tees Yard, Spring 1981)
The BBA class were very similar to the BAA type dealt with in the previous section but were longer vehicles and had a deeper underframe. Interestingly, they had a slightly lower g.l.w., at 74T. This was the largest modern air braked bogie bolster to be built in significant numbers. One vehicle was turned out in extended form, as the BLA, but this remained a one-off. Livery of 910460 is black overall with Flame Red ends and white lettering. (Ref: W9094/DL)

The BBA type was the big brother of the BAA and resembled it closely. None were given vacuum pipes when new. The prototype, 910000, appeared in 1973 and was followed by 910001 to 910120 in 1975/76. Due to cancellations in the building programme, the next to appear, in 1976/77, were numbered 910161 to 910491 (excluding 910366, which was built as the BLA 920000, mentioned in the caption above). Finally, a new batch, with detail differences, was being delivered during the review period. These were numbered 910492 to 910591.

For plate traffic, B.R. introduced three groups of vehicles, The SPA class were plate wagons of a completely new design. After two prototypes converted from Steel AB wagons (see Vol. 2, page 83), quite a large production run was built between 460002 to 461101, from 1979 to 1981. 460081 (opposite centre) illustrates the type..

For longer plates, eighty existing unfitted Boplate Es were refurbished as BPA wagons (see opposite upper). These were being delivered at the start of the review period and were numbered 965000 to 965079.

Finally, for out-of-gauge plates, fifty unfitted Trestle ED wagons were similarly refurbished as XVA wagons (opposite lower). These had appeared slightly earlier, the prototype, 990000, in 1977, and the production run, 990001 to 990049, in 1979.

With the exception of the BBA, none of these types had a long life in their intended traffic.

Top. ***965030 (Taken at Scunthorpe, Summer 1980)***
Steel plate was one product of British Steel, Scunthorpe, and all the vehicles on this page were recorded in a trip working from the works to the local yard. This vehicle was originally B947762 and of the type shown in Vol. 1, page 73. Livery is Flame Red with black underworks and white lettering.
(Ref: W8879/DL)

Centre. ***460081 (Taken at Scunthorpe, Summer 1980)***
The SPA design differed from previous practise in having three side sections rather than two, because they were longer than the traditional 15' 0" wheelbase vehicles (see section 8). Although perfectly adequate for their intended duties, most had a short life due to a lack of plate traffic. Livery is Flame Red with black underworks and white lettering
(Ref: W8872/DL)

Right. ***990005 (Taken at Scunthorpe, Summer 1980)***
The XVAs appeared in 1979 had the shortest lives of all the steel carriers. For those wanting to model this variety, this view shows the trestle construction to good effect, the livery being Flame Red with black underframe. Lettering was white and straps were blue. (Ref: W8880/DL)

Section 23. HAA Hoppers and Variants

250049 (Taken at Peak Forest, Summer 1982)
The home of the CBA hoppers was the Peak District of Derbyshire and this example is seen awaiting minor repairs. Compare this view with the one in Vol. 2, page 85, the opposite end of the vehicle is shown. In lime traffic the vehicles got very stained, as seen here. Livery is silver with Freight Brown bracing and black underworks. (Ref: W11495/DL)

The HAA merry-go-round coal hopper was one of the oldest air braked designs and a programme of body panel replacement began in the late 1970s. The rebodied vehicles could be identified by a row of bolts along the upper sides which were not found on original wagons. Less easy to spot was the lack of internal lateral braces at the top of the inside of the hopper. The original vehicles can be found in Vol. 2, pages 84 and 85.

The oldest vehicles were generally the first to be rebodied and 350054 (opposite upper) is one from the first batch built in 1965.

In addition to these, new vehicles began to appear at the start of the review period in 1980. These were numbered 365000 to 366129 and obviously had the row of bolts (mentioned above) from new. 365129 (opposite centre) is one of these.

The HAA code was retained for all the above vehicles but a new variant for 60 mph running, the HDA, appeared in 1982. This group of vehicles can be identified by the cylinder on top of the buffer beam at one end of the vehicle, a feature seen on the right of 368106 (opposite lower). The HDA class was numbered 368000 to 368459.

The CBA class (above) was the only other variant around at the time of the review period. The CDA clay wagons and the other variations will be dealt with in Volume 4 of this series.

350054 (Taken at Hartlepools, Autumn 1981)
HAA vehicles were always very dirty, due in part to the rubber tyred wheels which run along the bodysides in order to propel the vehicles through the loading plant. Thus, a shiny new vehicle always stood out in a train. Here two vehicles freshly out-shopped from BREL Shildon await their first load. The hopper sides are silver with the bracing in Flame Red, underworks are black and the lettering, white on black. (Ref: W8941/DL)

365129 (Taken at Worksop, Winter 1980)
Only the number range separates the rebodied stock from the new HAA fleet. As there was no space for a large batch at the end of the 35XXXX range, the new series commenced at 365000 and this is a fairly early vehicle from that batch. Livery is as above but the grime associated with the load is already apparent. (Ref: W8963/DL)

368106 (Taken at Hoo Junction, 1/8/82)
The HDA variant was introduced for higher speed running on longer workings. At least, when first delivered, the HDAs ran in train consists with HAAs, as seen here. Later they could be seen working in block formations made up of HDAs only. Livery is as above. (Ref: W11611/DL)

Section 24. 4 wheeled Scrap Wagons

ADC390001 (Taken at Basingstoke, 20/3/83)
The MFA scrap wagons built by B.R. were an adequate design that was a little ahead of its time. After a spell of use as barrier wagons and a longer time in store, they were used to convey scrap from B.R. works, such as Eastleigh, to steel works. As such they were deemed service vehicles, prefixed ADC and T.O.P.S. coded ZRA. Livery was Freight Brown with black underworks and white lettering. (Ref: W12970/DL)

The development of four wheeled scrap wagons was rather interesting. B.R. constructed the last two of the HBA hoppers (see Vol. 2, page 85) as MFA scrap wagons, as above. Numbered 390000 and 390001, they didn't really catch on because they were air braked and scrap was generally carried by vacuum braked 16T minerals when they were introduced.

The MFAs had leaf spring suspension, whereas RLS5900 (opposite upper), built in 1978 by Standard Wagon Ltd, introduced coil suspension to the design whilst keeping the same body shape. T.O.P.S. code was POA and the design code was PO010A.

RLS5900 was a prototype vehicle. A further batch of vehicles, RLS5901 to RLS5920, was built by Standard Wagon Ltd. in 1982. A different type of coil suspension was used but the main difference was the introduction of horizontal bracing to the bodywork, which presumably stopped bowing of the sides and ends. T.O.P.S. code was again POA and design code PO010B. RLS5901 (opposite centre) illustrates this group of vehicles.

With the contraction of the British steel industry, some relatively modern wagons became surplus to requirements. One such type was the PGA hoppers built for British Steel Ravenscraig (see page 65). The bodywork of these was removed and replaced by box bodies for scrap traffic. RLS5026 (opposite lower) is one of these. The bodywork was similar to RLS5901 but there was no side door. Numbers were RLS5000 to RLS5099 and design code PO014A.

Intriguingly, the story turns full circle because all the private owner vehicles seen on this page eventually became B.R. property (see Vol. 4).

RLS5900 (Taken at Brixton, Winter 1980)
Seen here in very clean condition for a scrap wagon, RLS5900 shows signs of wear on the end, indicating why perhaps the later vehicles had more bracing. Bound for the Sheerness steel works, which used scrap exclusively, it seems to have been recently repainted. Body is yellow with black underworks and lettering. (Ref: W10601/DL)

RLS5901 (Taken at Severn Tunnel Junction, 19/11/83)
The doors fitted to these early scrap wagons were to allow the floors to be cleaned out when necessary. They were dropped briefly after this batch but were later reintroduced. Livery of this batch was quite colourful but, due to the nature of the load, soon got very scruffy. Body, including solebar, was pale blue with yellow ends. Lettering was white. (Ref: W13540/DL)

RLS5026 (Taken at Tinsley Yard, 27/5/84)
The wagon above was observed in South Wales but, generally, these four-wheeled scrap wagons were to be found in the Sheffield area. These particular vehicles were allocated to British Steel, Aldwarke. Livery was again pale blue with yellow ends and white lettering. The SR stood for Standard Railfreight, a subsidiary of the builders. (Ref: W13983/DL)

Section 25. Private Owner Open and Steel Wagons

PR25511 (Taken at Northwich, 13/8/83)
This class is actually better described as a low-sided tippler wagon than a genuine open as there are no doors. The chassis were recovered from redundant 45T g.l.w. railtanks and fitted with modern suspension. Livery is light grey with black underworks and lettering. (Ref: W13203/DL)

Genuine open wagons, as in the Highfits of section 4 or the longer air braked wagons of section 16, were not a major part of the new private owner fleet but PR25511 (above) can loosely be grouped with such vehicles. Built in 1975 by Procor Ltd and using modernised 45T g.l.w. railtank chassis, the batch was numbered PR25500 to PR25523. T.O.P.S. code was PSA and design code PS016B/C, depending on which new springs were used. They have been used for salt traffic and also industrial lime in the north east of England.

Wagons for finished steel products were also rather rare. We looked at the Sheerness Steel bogie bolsters in Vol. 2, page 57 when they were new and we return to them with PR3003 (opposite upper). The first vehicle of the batch, PR3000, had already been converted to a bogie scrap wagon with box bodywork and it would not be long before the rest of them would follow.

British Steel, Corby had a requirement for wagons to carry pipes which could be unloaded without difficulty by fork lift trucks, traditional tube wagons being unsuitable since they needed a crane for unloading. They acquired a batch of timber wagons in 1971 from J. H. Davis Ltd of Lowestoft. These closely resembled the B.R. timber wagon and were vacuum braked. The batch of original vehicles was numbered BSCO4000 to BSCO4019 and T.O.P.S. code was PXV. BSCO4011 (opposite centre) illustrates this type.

Some of these vehicles were lengthened in 1975 and these vehicles were numbered BSCO4241 to BSCO4260, as illustrated by BSCO4242 (opposite lower). It was not considered worth upgrading them to air brakes and the whole fleet was withdrawn in 1986.

PR3003 (Taken at Sheerness, Summer 1980)
It was not only railtanks that were converted to new duties. The air braked bogie bolsters of Sheerness Steel, seen new in Vol. 2, are seen here stored, awaiting conversion to bogie scrap wagons with box bodies. Their finished products duties would be carried out by B.R. BDA wagons (see section 20). Livery was two-tone blue with black bogies. (Ref: W10767/DL)

BSCO4242 (Taken at Brierley Hill, 12/9/82)
The former timber wagons were a useful acquisition for British Steel, Corby, and, when they found a need for a longer wagon to take longer tubes, they had some converted. This one is loaded with the short tubes, however. Livery is as above. (Ref: W11856/DL)

BSCO4011 (Taken at Brierley Hill, 12/9/82)
B.R. found it expedient to designate certain goods yards as steel terminals and provide them with all the necessary heavy lifting equipment. Brierley Hill is one such near Wolverhampton. As seen here, P.O. wagons used them as well as B.R. stock. Livery is light grey with black underworks and white lettering.
(Ref: W11854/DL)

Section 26. Private Owner Bogie Tippler Wagons

BSSC26101 (Taken at Immingham Docks, 2/10/82)
Of all the bogie rotary tipplers operated by the various divisions of British Steel, the first batch, for Scunthorpe, were also the plainest in appearance. They were also the only one to have French bogies fitted, rather than British Steel's own design, as seen opposite. PR26101 is an outer vehicle and has a buffer beam at one end. Livery is dark grey with orange panels and black underworks. (Ref: W12148/DL)

Up until the early 1970s, imported iron ore was conveyed either in B.R. owned iron ore tippler wagons or hopper wagons. For the steel works that remained in use, new vehicles in the form of bogie tipplers which could be rotated without being uncoupled were developed.

First to appear were vehicles for British Steel, Scunthorpe and these were built by BREL Shildon in 1971. Inner vehicles, i.e. those with no buffer beams were numbered BSSC26000 to BSSC26094 and outer vehicles, i.e. those with a buffer beam at one end, were numbered BSSC26095 to BSSC26106, one of the latter being illustrated above.

Next to appear, in 1972, were vehicles for British Steel, Tees-side. These were built locally in 1972/73 by Redpath Dorman Long and had the distinctive BSC designed bogies. Inner vehicles were numbered BSTE26450 to BSTE26542 (opposite upper), whilst outer vehicles were numbered BSTE26543 to BSTE26563 (opposite centre). With the closure of this works, most of the vehicles passed into the ownership of Procor and were hired to Foster Yeoman Ltd for use in aggregate trains. The rest went on hire to ARC Ltd. but these received new numbers.

To supplement the vehicles transferred to aggregate use, 100T railtank chassis were rebuilt with box bodies. These were rather longer than the ex-BSTE wagons and had buffers at both ends. PR3145 (opposite lower) illustrates this class and is part of a batch numbered PR3140 to PR3149 which appeared in 1983.

PR26496 (Taken at South Croydon, 6/6/83)
These tipplers were transferred from iron ore traffic to aggregate traffic in 1981 and kept the old numbers, only the prefix changing from BSTE to PR to denote new ownership. The rotary facility on the couplings was made rigid as wagons were now unloaded by hydraulic grabs. Note the coupling release handle in this view of an inner vehicle. Livery is grey with Yeoman Blue and black bogies. (Ref: W13072/DL)

PR26561 (Taken at Crawley, 6/6/83)
The upsurge in aggregate traffic to locations in the South East meant that the ex-BSTE wagons soon found a new home. Crawley, Surrey only handled these tippler wagons and indeed continues to do so at the time of writing. This view shows the buffer beam of the outer wagon and livery is as above. (Ref: W13082/DL)

PR3145 (Taken at Crawley, 6/6/83)
Foster Yeoman required more vehicles than they received from BSTE, so they hired a batch of ten wagons which had been converted from 100T railtank chassis. They were lower in height than the ex-BSTE stock, and having buffers at both ends, could only be marshalled next to an outer BSTE wagon, as seen here. Livery is as above. (Ref: W13075/DL)

Section 27. Private Owner 4 wheeled Hoppers

PR8209 (Taken at Northwich, 14/2/82)
This design was one of the earliest to appear, being built by Standard Wagon Ltd. in 1971. Thus it was fitted with early pattern springs. Initially used by BP Chemicals on salt traffic, they had curved ends and ladders to suit, allowing staff to sheet the load. Livery is light grey with usual symbols. (Ref: W10521/DL)

Many of the four wheeled open hopper designs built for private owners were very distinctive in shape.

PR8209 (above) is one of a batch built by Standard Wagon Ltd. for salt traffic. The batch was PR8201 to PR8255, the T.O.P.S. code PGA and design code PG002D. Such traffic is very hard on wagons dedicated to it and the survivors were out of use some 10 years later. They would be refurbished, given modern springs and would pass into aggregate traffic.

BSTE18005 (opposite upper) was built by the same manufacturer but some four years later, in 1975. Designed to carry limestone from Redmire quarry to Lackenby steel works, Tees-side, there was obviously no perceived need for staff to climb on the wagons, as no ladders are fitted. The batch was numbered BSTE18000 to BSTE18114 with T.O.P.S. code PGA and design code PG010A. Surplus vehicles passed to wagon hirers in due course and were fitted with ladders, (see Vol. 4 of this series).

TAMC14861 (opposite centre) is contemporary with, but slightly older than, the aggregate hoppers found in Vol. 2, pages 54 and 55. Builder in this case was Procor Ltd. in 1979/80 and the batch was numbered TAMC14840 to TAMC14870. Design code was PG016G. As a lighter design, they have shields inside the ladders to protect the air brake equipment.

Finally, RLS6307 (opposite lower) has been included here, although its categorisation is difficult, since it is not a true 'hopper'. A box body with roller roof was fitted onto a chassis recovered from the ex-A.P.C.M. van fleet (see Vol.1, page 33). The batch of vehicles were coded PRA, design code PR001A, and numbered RLS6303 to RLS6316. They carried china clay from Cornwall to Scotland.

BSTE18005 (Taken at Tees Yard, Spr. 1981)
This design of limestone hopper was built with a specific traffic on a specific route in mind, namely Redmire Quarry to Teesside. Consequently they were not fitted with ladders as they were not deemed necessary for the job. They were also built for automatic discharge. Livery was light grey overall with red symbol and black lettering. (Ref: W10606/DL)

TAMC14861 (Taken at Brixton, Spr. 1980)
The condition of aggregate hoppers was usually pretty rough after only a short time in service. Tarmac, however, did seem to keep their wagons in fairly smart condition. Livery is white with green band and black or white lettering. The underworks are black. (Ref: W10963/DL)

RLS6307 (Taken at Tiverton Junction, 19/3/83)
These rebuilds were a very curious design They reused a 1960s chassis with original springing but were given air brakes, T.O.P.S. code being PRA. In the event not all were fully converted, and some had the basic box without ladders and roof (see Vol. 4). Livery was unusual also, the body being pale green with red roller roof. Underworks were black.
(Ref: W12948/DL)

Section 28. Private Owner 4 wheeled Covhops

BIS7831 (Taken at Castleton, 13/11/83)
Seen on delivery from Standard Wagon Ltd., Heywood, BIS7831 is one of the second type of PAA operated by British Industrial Sand from the Kings Lynn area. Livery is white with orange symbol and stripe and black name. Underworks are also black. (Ref: W13508/DL)

The stock working out of Middleton Towers which was examined in Sections 3, 5 and 7 was all elderly and, more to the point, not air braked. They were replaced by modern stock such as BIS7831 (above). This vehicle was part of the batch built in 1983 by Standard Wagon Ltd. Numbers were BIS7825 to BIS7844, T.O.P.S. code PAA and design code PA012A. The others were numbered between BIS7950 to BIS7989 and most were built by W. H. Davis Ltd.

TRL12800 (opposite upper) is one of a small batch of china clay covhops which worked between Cornwall and Central Scotland. This was another Standard Wagon Ltd. design, built in 1982 to design code PA010A. The batch was numbered TRL12800 to TRL12807.

During the early 1980s, Britain's nationalised steel works were closing and stock ordered to replace older B.R. stock had a remarkably short life. BSRV12569 (opposite centre) is one of the batch BSRV12500 to BSRV12599 which were jointly built by Procor, Wakefield and BREL Shildon in 1979. Being able to carry loads not affected by water, the roof could be left open and they were coded PGA rather than PAA. The example shown was one of a long line of stored wagons in 1984 and they were rebuilt in the same year as POA scrap wagons (see section 24).

Standard Wagon Ltd. were the builders of STET18715 (opposite lower) which was one of the batch STET18700 to STET18729. Built in 1981, these vehicles carried lime and thus always ran with the roof closed. T.O.P.S. code was PAA and design code was PA011A. This class were very similar to the BIS and BSRV wagons but the side plates for shunting purposes gave them a different look.

Of these covhop types, the Tullis Russell ones were to a special design because of tight curves at their destination and also because of the load, china clay. The others all have a strong family resemblance and it is rather surprising that the BSRV wagons did not apparently see any further main line use.

TRL12800 (Taken at Tiverton Junction, 19/3/83)
Operating between Cornwall and Markinch, Fife, these hoppers would have used the West Coast Main Line, usually in ones and twos. Livery is blue with blue name on white panel and black and maroon TRL symbol on yellow panel. Underworks was black. They soon got very stained with china clay, however, and often looked rather scruffy. (Ref: W12947/DL)

BSRV12569 (Taken at Castleton, 14/8/84)
These hoppers were dual purpose, designed to carry iron ore pellets from Glasgow Docks and limestone from Hardendale Quarries, Shap, to the now closed steel works at Ravenscraig. They were little used on these duties, apparently. Livery was light grey with black lettering and underworks. (Ref: W13334/DL).

STET18715 (Taken at Dewsnap Yard, Spring 1981)
Seen soon after delivery by the builders, this design was rather more rounded at the top than the others. The traffic was lime from Ferryhill, Co. Durham to Hartlepool and livery was off-white with black underworks. The nameplate was black on white. The large side plates very soon became soiled with horizontal black marks from the rubber wheels used to propel the vehicle through the loading plant. (Ref: W10602/DL)

Section 29. Private Owner Bogie Covhops (1)

RLS11803 (Taken at Standard Wagon, Heywood, 22/5/82)
As well as vehicles to carry powdered cement, some companies also required wagons to carry cement clinker. Clyde Cement operated from the Clitheroe, Lancs. works to Coatbridge, Scotland. Livery is light grey with blue and turquoise stripes and black CLYDE CEMENT. Solebar and bogies were also black. (Ref: W11549/DL)

The 1980s saw many new bogie covhop designs in operation, although some were rather short lived.

Clyde Cement was a new name which flourished briefly between Lancashire and Scotland. RLS11800 to RLS11814 were bogie clinker hoppers built in 1982 by Standard Wagon, where RLS11803 (above) is seen. Classified PBA, they had been de-roofed by 1990 and were re-classified PHA with a new design code of PH011A.

PR11309 (opposite upper) was built in 1972 by Charles Roberts Ltd. for tripolyphosphate traffic between Whitehaven and West Thurrock. They were still in this traffic during the review period but would soon pass on to other duties with a new livery. The batch was numbered PR11300 to PR11312, T.O.P.S. code was PBA and design code PB002A.

Rather more restricted in geographical territory were the potash wagons operating between Boulby Mine and Tees Docks with export traffic. STS11434 (opposite centre) was built in 1974 by Charles Roberts Ltd. as part of the batch STS11401 to STS11434. T.O.P.S. code was PBA and design code PB001B.

To replace older traditional stock on china clay traffic between Cornwall and the Potteries, French-built bogie hoppers, such as TRL11617, were delivered in 1982. The batch was TRL11600 to TRL11634, T.O.P.S. code, once again PBA and design code PB003A.

All the above hoppers were built for specific duties but, with the exception of the potash hoppers, could be seen running in ones and twos on SPEEDLINK services rather than in block trains.

Above. ***PR11309 (Taken at West Thurrock, Autumn 1980)***
The bogie tripolyphosphate hoppers hired by Proctor and Gamble represented one of the earlier bogie Covhop designs. At the time they were photographed they were due to be replaced by other vehicles on this traffic, only to re-emerge in the next review period (see Vol. 4). Livery was a very pale green, lettering was in black with black underframe.
(Ref: W10598/DL)

Centre. ***STS11434 (Taken at Tees Yard, Spring 1981)***
Probably having recently been overhauled at BREL Shildon, two potash covhops await return to Boulby mines. Livery is dark green with white name and side symbols, including the STS name. The second vehicle also has an orange stripe along the solebar.
(Ref: W10605/DL)

Right. ***TRL11617 (Taken at Tiverton Junction, 19/3/83)***
Seen recessed awaiting a path north, this SPEEDLINK train included three of these very distinctive wagons, as well as some of the PRAs seen on the previous page. Livery is white with blue stripe and main name. TIGER is in the usual black and yellow. Bogies and solebar are black, although the latter is well weathered with clay.
(Ref: W12944/DL)

Section 30. Private Owner Bogie Covhops (2)

TRL13501 (Taken at Whitemoor Yard, 11/3/84)
Many of the new generation of private owner wagons were very colourful. Some though were plainer, which at least made for easier painting. Built in France in 1982, this class of wagon, although small in numbers, seems to have travelled widely with various loads. Livery is dark grey with yellow and black Tiger symbol. (Ref: W13788/DL)

TRL13501 (above) represents a rather versatile class of wagon. Coded PBA under T.O.P.S. with Design code PB005A, the batch was numbered TRL13500 to TRL13524 and carried such loads as coal, sugarstone, agricultural lime, petroleum coke and calcified seaweed. In 1990, they were about to lose the roof and become open PHA hoppers.

We first examined the POLYBULK hopper in Vol. 2, pages 40 and 41. The term has come to cover a wide variety of different bogie designs. 21 88 099 8 042-6 (opposite lower) is a Belgian-owned vehicle dating from 1974/75 used for a variety of powder loads to and from the U.K. Later renumbered 33 88 938 0 000-X* to 33 88 938 0 110-X, they are quite common. One commodity they were originally used on was grain but they were later ousted from this traffic. T.O.P.S. code is IRB and design code is IRE442.

***** The 'X' denotes a computer check digit for data processing purposes, it varies from one wagon to the next and is not consecutive with wagon numbers.**

It was found that grain handling improved in hoppers with rounded sides, 33 70 938 5 015-0 (opposite centre) was one of a new class allocated specifically to that traffic and marked GRAINFLOW. These were English-owned by Traffic Services and were numbered 33 70 938 5 000-X to 33 70 938 5 029-X. As they were used for traffic in the U.K., T.O.P.S. code was PIB (changed later to JIB) rather than the 'I' prefix international code, and design code was JIE518. These were air braked and vacuum through piped.

To replace the four wheeled 'blues' hoppers (Vol. 1, pages 38 and 39) on the Scottish malt barley traffic, a similar type was introduced but it was not in POLYBULK livery. The shape of the body was also somewhat different. 33 70 928 0 017-2 (opposite top) illustrates this variant. The batch was numbered 33 70 928 0 000-X to 33 70 928 8 029-X. Being air braked only, T.O.P.S. code was PIA, later re-coded JIA and design code JIE538.

33 70 928 0 017-2 (Taken at Mossend Yard, 17/3/84)

The Scottish Malt Distillers fleet of bogie bulk grain wagons are rather more colourful. The main body is light grey with blue stripes and main panel with yellow symbols and lettering. Solebar and bogies are black. These vehicles would see seasonal use on the East Coast Main Line to various destinations in N.E. Scotland. (Ref: W13820/DL)

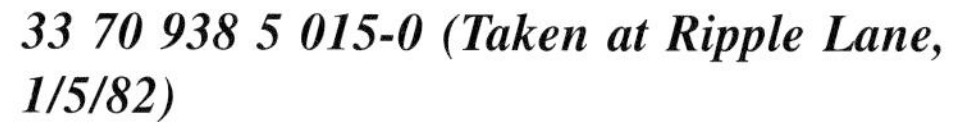

33 70 938 5 015-0 (Taken at Ripple Lane, 1/5/82)

The difference in shape between the flat Belgian type, one of which is to the left, and the rounded GRAINFLOW design is seen here. The whole of the side is green, ends and top being light grey. Solebar is yellow and bogies black. The two main names are yellow and the TSL symbol pink, black and white. (Ref: W11432/DL)

21 88 099 8 042-6 (Taken at Nunhead, Autumn 1981)

The 1974-built Belgian POLYBULK hoppers were more likely to be seen singly in a mixed SPEEDLINK train than some of the other types. Livery is light grey with green side panel and yellow name. Bogies were black and other lettering white. (Ref: W10408/DL)

Section 31. Private Owner 4 wheeled Powder (APCM)

STS10622 (Taken at Snodland, 1/7/83)
The 'Powderjet' design was a welcome change in shape for cement vehicles. The dark grey livery used on the new designs of APCM owned vehicles (opposite centre) was also used on these STS owned vehicles hired to APCM. This example also has a SULFACRETE plate, as seen in the centre photograph on the page opposite. APCM did not use these hired wagons for very long as its business was starting to contract. (Ref: W13094/DL)

The Associated Portland Cement Manufacturing Co. was Britain's largest cement producer and appropriately had the largest fleet of wagons.

One of the oldest types still in use were the old LA class (opposite top). Under T.O.P.S., these had been classified PCV and the design code was PC003A. Number series of these was APCM8500 to APCM8594 and the type illustrated is from the Metro-Cammell batch. The very similar Gloucester RCW vehicles were numbered APCM8300 to APCM8490 and the design code was PC001A.

The bulk of the APCM fleet was still made up of four-wheeled depressed centre wagons, as illustrated by APCM9388 (opposite centre). Being air braked, these vehicles were coded PCA and the design code was PC009A. APCM9100 to APCM9394 were built in the mid-1970s by BREL Shildon and BREL Doncaster, there being little to distinguish the two separate batches.

APCM10838 (opposite lower) was a one-off prototype PCA built in France to design code PC017A. It was followed by a small production batch numbered BCC10839 to BCC10849 and also by a hired batch, STS10600 to STS10651 (as above). Due to the vagaries of the B.R. system of issuing design codes by number block rather than actual design, these hired vehicles were PC017B, although no difference whatsoever can be detected.

APCM8560 (Taken at Hope Cement Works, 14/8/83)
In Vol. 1, page 32, we examined the early 1960s vintage LA bulk cement wagon. Although superseded on the longer runs by more modern stock, they could still be found during the review period, in this case at the Peak District cement works at Hope, near Sheffield. Note that no attempt is now made to advertise the company name, although the nameplate brackets still exist. Livery is now just cement dust with black lettering. (Ref: W13305/DL)

APCM9388 (Taken at Brixton, Summer 1981)
This view should be compared with the new wagon illustrated in Vol. 2, page 34. The big name plates must have been dust traps and have been removed. Instead, small plates indicate the grade of cement carried. These are yellow with red letters. Livery is light grey with black lettering.
(Ref: W10368/DL)

APCM10838 (Taken at Brixton, Sum. 1981)
One year into service for this French-built 'Powderjet' design. At about this time, the T.O.P.S. prefix letters for this fleet were changed to BCC for Blue Circle Cement. However, this first wagon still had the old code when photographed. The grey livery used here is a lot darker than on other cement vehicles and thus the lettering is in white. (Ref: W10650/DL)

Section 32. Private Owner 4 wheeled Powder (Other)

PR10013 (Taken at West Thurrock, Autumn 1980)
Proctor and Gamble used quite a number of different vehicles on the Whitehaven soap powder traffic. PR10013 dates from 1976 and is one of a number that were then on hire to that company. Livery was lime green with black solebar. The Procor branding is the usual blue on white. (Ref: W10599/DL)

Apart from the A.P.C.M. fleet, there were still quite a few other companies operating cement wagons. PR10013 (above) is not, in fact, being used for cement traffic, it is on tripolyphosphate traffic from Whitehaven to West Thurrock. It should be compared with PR10008 (Vol. 2, page 73) as it is ostensibly of the same batch, PR10000 to PR10018, built in 1976 by Procor Ltd. There are subtle detail differences, as well as with the livery.

PR9406 (opposite upper) also bears some resemblance to PR10013 but it was built a few years earlier in 1973 by the same firm then known as Charles Roberts Ltd. Built for cement traffic, it also has ladders and catwalks. The batch ran from PR9400 to PR9424 and being air braked, they were coded PCA. The design code was PC010A.

RBL10419 (opposite centre) is operated by Ribble Cement from their Clitheroe, Lancs., cement works and was built by Standard Wagon Ltd. in 1977. Air braked, as can be seen, they were coded PCA and the design code was PC013B. The batch was numbered RBL10400 to RBL10443.

Finally, RLS10321 (opposite lower) is representative of the latest design seen awaiting delivery at Standard Wagon Ltd., in 1983. Design code was PC013C and the batch ran from RLS10300 to RLS10344, some of which were later lettered CASTLE CEMENT. Note that neither these nor the Ribble wagons have access ladders although they do have catwalks. These replaced the Presflo wagons, as seen in Vol. 2, page 33.

Right. ***PR9406 (Taken at Nunhead, Summer 1981)*** *These vehicles were operating between the Rugby cement works at Halling, Kent and Southampton. They had replaced B.R. Presflos (Vol. 2, page 32) in this traffic. Livery was grey with black solebar. The Procor logo is red, black and white and the Rugby plate black and orange. (Ref: W10357/DL)*

Centre. ***RBL10419 (Taken at Clitheroe, 23/5/82)*** *These cement wagons operated to Middlesborough, although one turned up in Kent when brand new in an exhibition train. Livery, under all the cement dust was grey with black solebar. The Ribble symbol, totally obliterated here, was a castle in red with the words RIBBLE and CEMENT in white. (Ref: W11581/DL)*

Below. ***RLS10321 (Taken at Standard Wgn., Heywood, 13/11/83)*** *Probably the last time it would ever be clean, this vehicle stands at the works where it was built. It closely resembles the vehicle above but there are minor differences. Livery is grey with black solebar. The 'T' symbol is red and TUNNEL CEMENT is black. (Ref: W13416/DL)*

Section 33. Private Owner Railtanks (Shell Mex and B.P. - 1)

BPO37271 (Taken at Stoke-on-Trent, 12/8/83)
Refurbished Class A 45T railtanks in the BP Oils fleet were renumbered into a new series, this example having previously been BPO65767. At this time, the rules regarding liveries for class A tanks were still current and livery remained grey with red solebar. (Ref: W13157/DL)

As mentioned in Vol. 2, the Shell Mex and B.P. companies decided to split their tank fleet just prior to the introduction of T.O.P.S. in 1973 and by the 1980s most tanks at least bore T.O.P.S. plates with the new owner code, BPO for B.P. Oils Ltd. and SUKO for Shell (U.K.) Oils Ltd.

BPO50161 (opposite above) was one example of a batch of smaller capacity vehicles which was split up. The B.P. Oils vehicles were numbered from BPO50160 to BPO50167 and the Shell ones from SUKO50100 to SUKO50112. All had been built in 1964 by Charles Roberts Ltd. and were coded TTV under T.O.P.S. Being vacuum braked, they would soon be up for withdrawal.

The BP Oils Ltd. fleet also included refurbished 45T tanks with new springs and air brakes only. Some of these were also renumbered into a new series BPO37060 upwards, for diesel traffic, and, as can be seen above, the recent trend not to display a company logo was reversed when the tanks passed through a main workshop, in this case Marcroft Ltd. In time, all 45T railtanks still running would be re-sprung.

Bogie railtanks, although less popular, continued in use. Some were transferred to new owners or refurbished and even a few new examples were built (see section 37).

SUKO80108 (opposite centre) is a Class A railtank dating from the 1967/68 period and the original Shell Mex and B.P. fleet. It was air braked only and coded TEA under T.O.P.S. It would soon be surplus to requirements and would be withdrawn, the chassis being re-used on a bogie open gravel wagon.

SUKO83304 (opposite centre) is a lagged Class B fuel oil tank and had a similar history. Although obviously having received some attention in the shops recently, it would also be disposed of fairly soon and the chassis be re-used.

It should be noted, though, that SHELL U.K. were more prone to dispose of their railtank fleet than were B.P. Oils. Similar vehicles could be seen operating for the latter company for a lot longer.

Right. ***BPO50161 (Taken at Hoo Junction, Summer 1981)***
Shell Mex and B.P. Ltd. did not have many four wheeled tanks smaller than the standard 45T g.l.w. size but did have a small number of tanks for lubricating oil built in 1964. To these were added the Lubricant Producers fleet. Livery of BPO50161 is black with white lettering.
(Ref: W10366/DL)

Centre. ***SUKO80108 (Taken at Stanlow, 13/2/82)***
The 100T bogie Class A railtank for petrol had been around for roughly fifteen years when this view was taken but, although still relatively modern, its days were numbered. This very grubby example is in standard grey livery with red half-solebar and black bogies.
(Ref: W10546/DL)

Below. ***SUKO83304 (Taken at Stanlow, 13/2/82)***
This heavy fuel oil tank would soon meet a similar fate to 80108 above, but it has been through the shops recently to have the lagging attended to, hence the patch painting. Livery is all black with white lettering on sides and ends.
(Ref: W10546/DL)

Section 34. Private Owner Railtanks (Shell Mex and B.P. - 2)

SUKO71508 (Taken at Warrington, Old Walton Jct., 20/2/82)
Bitumen railtanks require heat to make the commodity fluid enough to enable loading and discharge. Thus they are lagged to keep the load as warm as possible during transit. Despite this, they still need special heat treatment when it comes to discharging and the two circular ports on the lower tank end are needed for this purpose. By the mid 1970s, certain firms were taking modern four wheeled railtanks into stock. This is a slightly later example, being built in 1981, but is typical of these vehicles. Livery is black with a yellow end cone and white lettering. (Ref: W10583/DL)

New types of bitumen car appeared just prior to, and during, the review period, as illustrated by SUKO71508 (above) and purchased by Shell U.K. from W.H. Davis Ltd. in 1981. The batch was SUKO71501 to SUKO71515 and the tanks were air braked only. T.O.P.S. code was TUA and design code was TU006B. They operated from Stanlow to Exeter or Elswick (Newcastle).

Older examples could still be seen, as SUKO52508 (opposite above), still carrying its old S.M. & B.P. number of 9850. (All of this type seem to have been transferred to Shell at the time of the split). It falls in the number range SUKO52400 to SUKO52636, which was covered by numerous builders, this one was built by Charles Roberts Ltd. about 1971 and vacuum braked only with TTV T.O.P.S. code. It appears to have been withdrawn by the late 1980s.

SUKO59501 (opposite centre) is an L. P. G. tank from the number range SUKO59400 to SUKO59650, once again built by various companies in 1966/67. It has received some refurbishment, such as air brakes and tank protector plate above the buffer beam, but the springs are original. T.O.P.S. code was TTA. This one was soon withdrawn but others were later re-sprung, as BPO59161 (opposite lower) which dates from the same period. It has been fitted with Gloucester pedestal suspension in addition to other modern features, and was still in regular use in 1990 as part of the batch BPO59160 to BPO59167.

SUKO52508 (Taken at Stanlow, 13/2/82)
Bitumen railtanks were always very dirty and this one is no exception. Despite the appearance of newer types, SUKO seemed less interested than BPO in using rail and rather ran its fleet down. Livery is, of course, black with white lettering. (Ref: W10537/DL)

SUKO59501 (Taken at Stanlow, 13/2/82)
By contrast, L.P.G. tanks were usually very clean, although this one appears to have been in the workshops recently. Livery is white, including the tank protector, with orange band and black solebar. It may just be ex-works, with barrier wagons on either side. (Ref: W10492/DL)

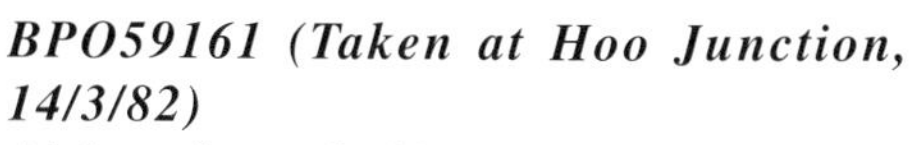

BPO59161 (Taken at Hoo Junction, 14/3/82)
Although probably built by the same manufacturer as SUKO59501, the provision of pedestal suspension makes a big difference to the appearance of the vehicle. Livery is as above. Although this tank has a lamp bracket, oil burning tail lamps, still in widespread use at the time, could not have been attached. (Ref: W10444/DL)

Section 35. Private Owner Railtanks (Other - 1)

STS53209 (Taken at Dewsnap Yard, Spring 1981)
The carbon dioxide (CO_2) tanks lasted for a long time on the B.R. system and some of them, such as this example which by this time was quite old, were given updated running gear. Compare this example with the one from the same batch, in Vol. 2, page 75, in particular the state of the white/orange livery. (Ref: W10603/DL)

At the start of the review period the Charrington, Gardner, Lockett railtank fleet still had in use some very early vacuum braked railtanks built in 1963. As can be seen in the photograph (opposite upper), they were a lot smaller when compared with the later 45T g.l.w. tanks, but shared the monobloc tank mount design. Being vacuum braked only, they did not survive much longer and were appearing on their final outings before withdrawal.

Not so, however, for some other 1960s types, such as the STS-owned CO_2 railtanks hired by Distillers. These were given new suspension, in this case Gloucester pedestal type, and the brakegear was revised where necessary from vacuum braked to air braked and vacuum through piped. Soon the vacuum piping would disappear, but the tanker fleet would carry on in service to the end of the review period and far beyond.

Other types built in the late 1960s received a complete overhaul during the early 1980s. A line of caustic soda tanks is seen (opposite centre) after a repaint. Interestingly, the tank protectors have been fitted above the headstocks but the suspension has not been upgraded. In contrast, TRL70724 (opposite lower) was a caustic soda liquor tank owned by Tiger Rail and hired to I.C.I. Mond. It was built by Standard Wagon in 1977. The batch was TRL70700 to TRL70727 and they were air braked only, T.O.P.S. code TUA, and design code TU013A. As seen here, these vehicles were operating from Runcorn but they passed to other operators later.

Above. ***CGL53701 (Taken at West Thurrock, Autumn 1980)***
The type of tank illustrated here is an interesting survivor in the review period and was the halfway point in development between the 1958 ESSO cars, which had tanks of a similar size, and the 1964 monobloc style 45T g.l.w. tanks. Livery is black with white lettering. (Ref: W10939/DL)

Centre. ***TRL51644 (Taken at Runcorn, 20/2/82)***
Perhaps on their first journey after refurbishment, this line of very clean caustic soda tanks is very impressive. Livery is I.C.I. blue/green with orange solebar, a peculiarity of that company, and all symbols are clearly seen. (Ref: W10717/DL)

Right. ***TRL70724 (Taken at Northwich, 14/2/82)***
A feature of the new caustic soda railtanks was the protection plate fitted at either end above the headstocks. In minor accidents, this prevented the buffers striking the tank barrel. Many other hazardous tanks types received these features and older examples were retro-fitted. This example is well weathered with the yellow Tiger Rail transfer being barely visible. (Ref: W10757/DL)

Section 36. Private Owner Railtanks (Other - 2)

23 70 719 2 285-8 (Taken at Brixton, Summer 1981)
Long before the days of lead-free petrol, anti-knock compound was sent from the U. K. to many European oil refineries. It was usually conveyed in the tank fleet of the Associated Octel company and illustrated here is one of the 1950s built ferry tanks bound for Dover and the Continent. Livery is grey with black solebar and white or black lettering. The OCTEL symbol has a blue section. (Ref: W10370/DL)

One example of an Associated Octel ferry tank appears in Vol. 2, page 71. The one illustrated above was also British-built but was older. Built in 1954, they were about to be relegated to internal U.K. use and would be renumbered AO48462 to AO48491. None would be in use by 1990.

In Vol. 1, page 81, a BP Chemicals railtank was featured. STS53020 (opposite upper) represents the same class of vehicle 10 years later on Phthalate Ester traffic. The batch was STS53012 to STS53061 and they were built in 1963 by Powell Duffryn. Being vacuum-braked only, they were T.O.P.S. coded TTV and would not see much further service. Mention has been made earlier of the differing types of end ladder on the four wheeled railtanks. This was dictated by the user in a lot of cases. Thus STS53020 has an elaborate ladder system and safety rails on top of the tank. That fitted to ALG49128 (opposite centre) looks positively dangerous by comparison.

Carless, Capel and Leonard were a company dealing in solvents extracted during the oil refining process and their tanks were regularly seen at B.P. Isle of Grain. ALG49128 (opposite centre) is from the batch numbered ALG49087 to ALG49253, not all of which were used by Carless. The builder was R. Y. Pickering in 1965. These particular tanks are vacuum braked, but because they have the A.F.I. variant, they are T.O.P.S. coded TTF.

TRL70728 (opposite centre) was a petrol railtank which, for reasons unknown, seems to have had a very short working life. Built in 1977 by Procor Ltd., they were owned by Tiger Rail and hired to Esso. By 1980, all were stored out of use. The batch was TRL70728 to TRL70733 and the vehicles were air braked and vacuum through piped. T.O.P.S. code was TUB and design code TU014A.

Not many of these elderly vehicles used by the smaller companies would survive any length of time. Only those operated by the large companies, with the funds to do it, would be refurbished with new springs and have the vacuum brakes replaced with air brakes.

STS53020 (Taken at Burry Port, Sum. 1981)
A TTV specialist chemical tank in rather grubby condition after nearly 20 years more or less continuous service. Grey with red solebar, the BP shield was the usual gold on green and CHEMICALS was in blue. (Ref: W10376/DL)

ALG49128 (Taken at Hoo Junction, Summer 1981)
When built, this railtank was originally hired to ESSO for the transport of petrol and was observed on that traffic in 1970. It is not known when it passed to Carless, livery remained grey with red solebar, however. Other tanks in this batch had been in the Carless traffic throughout their career. The Carless symbol is pink on white. (Ref: W10365/DL)

TRL70728 (Taken at Standard Wagon, Reddish, Summer 1980)
For the whole batch to have been found stored out of use only three years after being built suggests there must have been a serious problem with these tanks. Even if ESSO, the first hirer, didn't want them surely some other user would have been found. Livery is usual Class A paint scheme. (Ref: W10731/DL)

Section 37. Private Owner Railtanks (Bogie)

STL85707 (Taken at Warrington, Old Walton Jct., 14/2/82)
This bogie tank is rather a rare mix of styles. Built in France in 1970, it has B.R. Gloucester bogies. The batch was STL85703 - 08/10 and, as can be seen, they were air braked. T.O.P.S. code was TEA and design code TE004A. Livery at this stage was turquoise tank barrel with white lettering and black bogies. (Ref: W11277/DL)

As mentioned in section 33, bogie oil and petrol tanks were becoming unpopular, but a reversal of this general trend saw the building of RLS82209 (opposite top) in 1980. The batch was RLS82200 to RLS82213 and they were air braked TEAs. Design code was TE009B and they operated from Lindsey Oil refinery for Total Petroleum.

TRL78804 (opposite centre) is one of a small batch of five tanks, TRL78800-04, built in 1975 by the French company C.F.M.F., Balbigny. Owned by Tiger Railcar Leasing, they were designated Class B railtanks and their original hirer was Crosfield of Warrington, the tanks being painted in the Crosfield turquoise livery. By 1983 they were hired to English China Clay for slurry traffic but had not been repainted.

8017 (opposite lower) has proved difficult to identify because none of my sources mention Albright and Wilson. If my guess is correct, this is one of the batch STS86050 to STS86062 built by BREL Ashford in 1971. These tanks were air braked and vacuum through piped, as this is, and had the T.O.P.S. code of TDB. Design code was TD007A.

Finally, some modern tanks were being re-used by other operators. STL85707 (above) is a bogie sulphuric acid tank built in 1970 and originally hired to Leathers Chemicals. By the time of the photograph, Hays Chemicals was the operator, although the vehicles still carried the former name.

Opposite Centre. ***TRL78804 (Taken at Tiverton Junc., 19/8/81)***
Wagons in china clay traffic were generally painted in lighter colours so that load spillage is not too obvious. The fact that TRL78804 is not so painted lends credence to the theory that it was not built for such traffic originally. The top catwalk safety rails are very typical of a French design. (Ref: W12946/DL)

Above. ***RLS82209 (Taken at Dewsnap Yard, Spring 1981)***
This view forms an interesting comparison with SUKO80108 on page 75, showing what design changes had been made in 14 years. The chief one must be the use of a continuous solebar instead of the type used on the earlier vehicle. The bogies are modern too, Gloucester GPS pattern. Livery is, of course the usual Class A grey with red solebar and black bogies. TOTAL is in black. (Ref: W10604/DL)

Right. ***8017 (Taken at Worksop, Winter 1980/81)***
This is a good example of why notes should always be taken. Although very similar to the anhydrous ammonia tank in Vol. 2, page 78, it isn't the same. The hirer is Albright and Wilson, Marchon Division but because it carries a pre-T.O.P.S. number of 8017 it has been difficult to identify. It is possibly a Vinyl Chloride Monomer railtank built in 1971 by BREL Ashford. Livery is the standard white with orange band and black underworks. (Ref: W10600/DL)

Section 38. Continental Ferry Vans

21 80 579 5 004-8 (Taken at Hoo Jct., 1/8/82)
At first sight, just an ordinary four wheeled continental ferry, but the above vehicle is, in fact, an example of German ingenuity. The doors at both ends can be opened and the roof can slide outwards to allow loading by crane. Built in 1965 and given Diagram number IME277, these vans were dual air and vacuum braked and coded IMX under T.O.P.S. Livery is German Railways brown with white lettering. (Ref: W11605/DL)

Having been featured in Vols. 1 and 2 of this series, we return for a further look at ferry vans, which remained a prominent feature of freight operations throughout the period covered by the whole series.

The Germans had ever been innovative in wagon design and their sliding roof van of the mid-1960s was considered a great breakthrough. B.R. even converted two tube wagons to have similar features but it does not appear as if that idea flourished. 21 80 579 5 004-8 (above) shows the features of the design well but only one seems to have been on international duties by 1990.

The Belgians progressed the German theme in the late 1970s and produced a rather different and very angular vehicle. The roof was rolled to one end, rather than split in the middle, and it was flexible, unlike the German design, which had rigid roof panels. There were no end doors but the sides were split into two large panels which could be opened. 21 88 579 9 006-1 (opposite upper) shows the flat end of the type; the other end had the roof operating mechanism. All of these remained in service in 1990.

Recent events in the Balkans have put the former Yugoslavia into the spotlight. Before the break-up, the State operated vans to the U.K. and 21 72 214 0 210-0 (opposite centre) is one of these. Actually built in Germany in the 1960s, it has that country's design features.

Finally, bogie ferry vans were beginning to appear. 21 80 029 8 055-3 (opposite lower) is one of the early designs which was built in 1977. Given Diagram IWE 476, they were owned by Cargowaggon and were air-braked and vacuum through piped.

Right. ***21 88 579 9 006-1 (Taken at Warrington, Arpley, 3/10/82)***
Built in 1977 and given Diagram ILE 479, these vehicles were air braked and vacuum through piped, being T.O.P.S. code ILB. Livery was Belgian Railways brown with white lettering on black panels. (Ref: W12245/DL)

Centre. ***21 72 214 0 210-0 (Taken at Nunhead, Summer 1981)***
The Yugoslavian vans of Diagram IME 199, being German built, were rather hard to pick out in a line of similar ferry vans. The livery was also brown, which did not help, but it was of a rather darker shade than the Belgian, French or German vehicles. These vans were dual air and vacuum braked and coded IMX under T.O.P.S. (Ref: W10362/DL)

Below. ***21 80 029 8 055-3 (Taken at St. Blazey, Summer 1981)***
Bogie ferry vans would become a very familiar sight on B.R. as the review period progressed but they were not that common at the beginning. They were generally of German origin in the early days and this example was built in 1977 to Diagram IWE 476. The vacuum through pipe is obvious in this view and, being air braked also, they were T.O.P.S. coded IWB. The livery was silver with blue ends and black underworks. Lettering was brown on yellow. (Ref: W10386/DL)

Section 39. Continental Ferry Railtanks

21 87 079 8 979-2 (Taken at Aylesbury, 9/5/82)
Identifying foreign railtanks is sometimes rather difficult because records are scarce and most of them were renumbered in the late 1980s. This particular example, allocated to wine traffic, also seems to have changed owners, as it is listed as being owned by Fert and Co. Livery when photographed was grey with white name on red rectangle and black bogies. (Ref: W7756/DL)

In the 1960s/1970s period, foreign owned railtanks did appear but they were usually four wheeled. By the 1980s, bogie designs began to appear regularly.

One commodity not previously carried but coming into prominence was wine. 21 87 079 8 979-2 (above) was one of two, to Diagram ICE441, for this traffic (later renumbered to 33 87 789 0 612-X). It had air brakes and vacuum through pipes, being coded ICB under T.O.P.S. Build date was probably 1981.

21 87 079 8 018-9 (opposite upper) was one of 16 built in 1979 to Diagram ICE496. Owned by French company NACCO, these vehicles operated between Ellesmere Port and Europe, suggesting a liquid chemical load. The other logo, POLYSAR, tends to confirm this. This class was air braked only, being T.O.P.S. coded ICA.

33 87 789 6 013-6 (opposite centre) is a rather shorter tank but uses the same bogie type. Again, the load is not specified and such records as exist do not even name a British destination. The location of the tank when photographed would suggest Ellesmere Port once more and a chemical load. Four were built in 1983 to Diagram ICE541 and all were air braked only, the T.O.P.S. code being ICA.

Four wheeled tanks did still appear but they were comparatively vintage. 23 80 739 4 006-2 (opposite lower) is one of a batch of eight built in 1965 to Diagram ICE633. As was usual for that period, air brakes and vacuum through pipes were fitted and the T.O.P.S. code was IBB. The hirer was I.C.I. Mond and dangerous chemicals were conveyed from Runcorn to various European destinations.

One common factor linking all the tanks shown in this section is the fact that they had come from or were destined for Europe. This meant that all would pass along the narrow corridor from the train ferry at Dover to the cross-London lines through Clapham Junction and Kensington Olympia. During the review period, they would be marshalled in SPEEDLINK trains.

21 87 079 8 018-9 (Taken at Brixton, Summer 1981)
Taken from a useful high angle, this view shows top detail of a fairly common sight in the 1980s. Two tanks are seen here on their way to the Dover train ferry. The tank is grey, the NACCO symbol red/blue with white lettering and the POLYSAR symbol yellow on black. (Ref: W10375/DL)

33 87 789 6 013-2 (Taken at Warrington, Arpley, 26/5/84)
Although much shorter than the other two French-built bogie railtanks, this example is much more substantial, even having two end platforms. Livery is white with black underparts. The owner is Lorcatransport in fact. Thann et Mulhouse is the hirer and this symbol is black on yellow. (Ref: W13911A/DL)

23 80 739 4 006-2 (Taken at Dewsnap Yard, Spring 1981)
As it is somewhat off route, this tank may have been for repairs when recorded. All German ferry tanks built in the 1960s are rather angular and this example is no different. As it carries dangerous liquids, it is in the obligatory white livery with horizontal orange band. The solebar is black and the VTG symbols are dark grey.

(Ref: W10980/DL)

Section 40. P. W. Hopper Wagons (Traditional)

DB983808 (Taken at Tonbridge West Yard, Spring 1980)
With the delivery of new bogie SEA COW ballast hoppers (see section 43), many of the early B.R. designs, such as the MACKEREL on the right of this view, began to be phased out. The later types, such as the CATFISH and the DOGFISH, in the second line, lasted into the 1990s. DB983808 is in Olive Green livery, as are all the other ballast hoppers seen. (Ref: W9760/DL)

The various designs of four wheeled ballast hopper were developed from pre-W.W.II practice. Those with end platforms stemmed from a Metropolitan Cammell design, which B.R. called the TROUT (see Vol. 1, page 90). This had three chutes, one for between the rails and the other two for either side of the rails.

The B.R. ZMV MACKEREL design was smaller, 17T as opposed to 25T, and had only the central chute. It was also vacuum-braked but retained the same characteristics, being built by Metropolitan Cammell in 1951/52. The type is illustrated by DB992264 (opposite upper), numbers DB992247 to DB992380. Only four survived in 1989.

The ZEV CATFISH (above and opposite centre) was the B.R. version of the MACKEREL. Slightly larger at 19T, it also had welded bodywork. Numbers were DB983376 to DB983576, DB983627 to DB983896 (which had OLEO hydraulic buffers and roller bearings), DB992531 to DB992710 and DB993508 to DB993566. Most survived in 1989.

The B.R. ZFV DOGFISH was the standard version of the TROUT and its close B.R. built relative, the Diagram 1/584 HERRING. Capacity was reduced to 24T and the construction was again welded. Numbers of these were DB983000 to DB983309 and DB992711 to DB993507 (oil axleboxes and self-contained buffers) and DB983577 to DB983626, DB983897 to DB983920 and DB993567 to DB993634 (roller bearings and OLEO hydraulic buffers). In addition, DB993471 to DB993507 and DB993595 to DB993634 were allocated to the S.R. originally and were fitted with wide outer chutes, to clear the third rail (type not illustrated).

DB983251 (opposite lower) does illustrate another variant, dating from 1962. Ballast hoppers operating from Santon Slag depot, Scunthorpe, with slag ballast, which is less dense than granite ballast, were given upwardly-extended sides and ends to take a greater volume.

DB992264 (Taken at Normanton, Winter 1980/81)
Traditional ballast hopper trains in the review period exhibited quite a high degree of variety when compared with the bogie hopper trains. The MACKEREL seen here was the least common type but worthy of a model. Livery is black with original straw lettering and T.O.P.S. code ZMV in white. (Ref: W9812/DL)

DB992649 (Taken at Normanton, Winter, 1980/81)
The much cleaner lines of the B.R. design are well illustrated in this view. This CATFISH is a somewhat older vehicle than DB983808 (opposite) and it is rather surprising that it has retained all the lettering on the right when it has been repainted Olive Green. (Ref: W9761/DL)

DB983251 (Taken at Normanton, Winter 1980/81)
The strong family resemblance between DOGFISH and the CATFISH, above, is well shown here. Note the operating instructions pertaining to the wheels painted on the end extension of the vehicle to the left; not usually possible on these early hoppers. Note that none of the hoppers shown have been modernised with roller bearings, etc. This came much later. Livery is Olive Green but without correct ZFV code. (Ref: W9897/DL)

Section 41. P. W. Open and Rail (Traditional)

DB988066 (Taken at Briton Ferry, Summer 1981)
The period covered by this volume was the last in which the older designs, such as the ZCO LING seen here, could be seen. DB988066 is even in the relatively rare P.W. Red livery from the late 1950s/early 1960s period, although with modern lettering. (Ref: W9801/DL)

As the spread of trains with automatic brakes progressed across the network, the review period saw the gradual concentration of the unfitted traditional designs into smaller and smaller areas.

Some types were eliminated altogether. The 14T ZCO LING (above) was an original G.W.R. design that had been adopted by B.R. One batch of 200 vehicles, numbered DB988000 to DB988199, had been built in 1949/50 and they had served in most parts of the country, along with similar G.W.R.-built stock.

The 40T YLO GANE A was another design which had a similar history to the LING. Illustrated also in Vol. 1, page 95, DB996702 (opposite lower) was part of the batch DB996700 to DB996803 built in 1949/50. Only two survived in 1989.

The 20T YCO PILCHARD (opposite centre) had different origins but was another early type dating from 1950/51. It was an L.N.E.R. design but not built before 1948. Numbered DB990050 to DB990099, they did not stray very far from ex-L.N.E.R. territory. The vehicle illustrated was the last one recorded.

The unfitted GRAMPUS (opposite upper) was, of course, much more numerous. Many thousands, numbered DB984000 to DB984993, DB985000 to DB986986 and DB990100 to DB990958, had been built between 1951 and 1958 and, although some had begun to be modified (see section 42 for some examples), the vast bulk of them remained in the condition illustrated.

Opposite centre. ***DB990072 (Taken at Doncaster, Winter 1980/81)***
Possibly awaiting condemnation and scrapping, this PILCHARD was the last I recorded. Of the total of 50 built, I managed to photograph ten - not bad for such a rare type! The paint on this one has flaked away but it would have been black. The PILCHARD code is just about legible. (Ref: W9818/DL)

Opposite Lower. ***DB996702 (Taken at Tees Yard, Spring 1981)***
The GANE A was a G.W.R. design and generally, they tended to stick to that region. As seen in Vol. 1, they began to wander in the late 1960s and this increased in the 1970s, when the S.R. went all-fitted. However, this example may have been destined for BREL Shildon for some reason. Livery was indecipherable under the all the dirt! (Ref: W9775/DL)

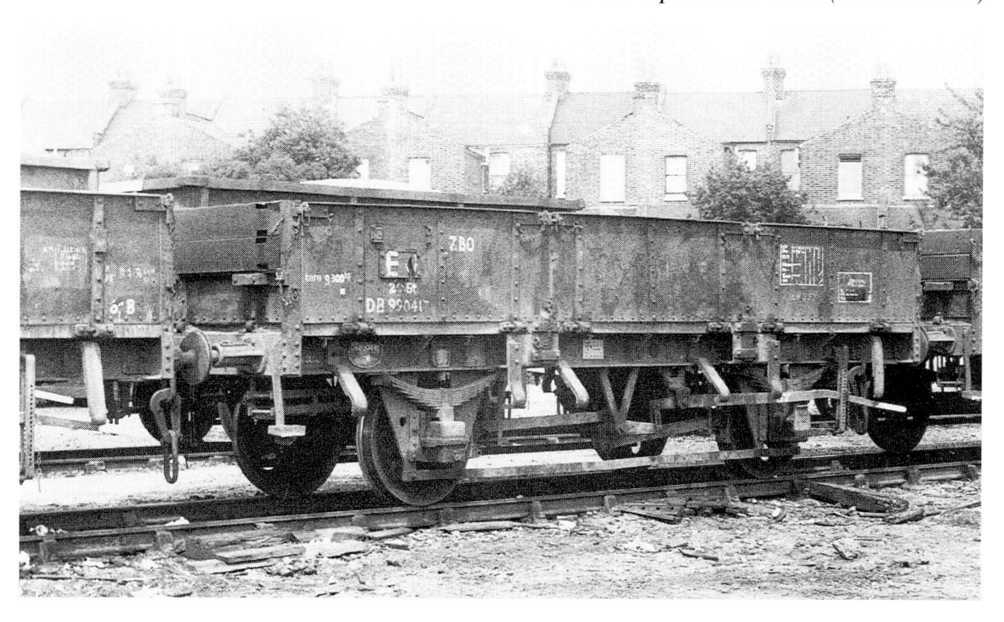

Right. ***B990417 (Taken at Leyton P.W. Depot, Spr. 1980)***
This is one of the 1953-built vehicles and is in virtually original condition. The Ew plate which was used on this type to denote regional allocation is still in position but there is no paint. The ZBO T.O.P.S. code has been applied, however. (Ref: W9603/DL)

Section 42. P. W. Open Wagons (Refurbished)

DB726462 (Taken at Battersea Yard, Summer 1981)
Traditionally, wagons which carried ballast had drop sides and ends. However, by the 1980s, renewal of track usually involved a process called deep digging, which required a new ballast bed upon which to lay the track. Hopper wagons were not the ideal wagon for such duties and the method of unloading the ballast, by mechanical grab, required solid sides and ends. The conversion by the Southern Region of redundant SHOCHOOD B and COIL L wagons started a trend which is still current today. DB726462 is in Olive Green livery. (Ref: W9767/DL)

The first DACE conversions (above) began to appear in 1981 and they have only just been replaced by improved conversions. Basically all that was done was to strip out the interior and stop the body from moving, as the source vehicle, the SHOCHOOD B, had been shock absorbing. Exactly how many were converted is unclear at the time of writing but my photographic collection of the type is over 50 between DB726226 to DB726519. They were originally coded ZDV but this later became ZCV DACE. They seem to have been used only on the S.R.

The early LAMPREY conversions, as illustrated by DB991259 (opposite upper), do not seem to have been numerous. DB991156 was observed at Darlington and remained unfitted. DB991244/59/61/7/90/2 were all observed on the S.R. and had been vacuum-braked. Additionally; at least one was later recorded as a ZCV CRAB and this could be considered an interim stage.

It is believed that only four B.R.-built 12T SOLE were given air brakes for the Merseyrail system and these were coded ZCA. The numbers were DB982005/54, DB982120 and DB982223 (opposite centre). Only DB982054 remained in service in 1989.

The GRAMPUS wagons given through air pipes were all originally unfitted and were rather more numerous than the ZCA SOLE. They were coded ZBQ and known numbers are DB984335/7/48, DB986171/82/5/92, DB986201/5/9/15/6/222/3/4/32/45/6/7/68/73/84/91/4, DB986300/1/20/2/3/4/7/31/2/5 and DB986914. Two of these vehicles are illustrated (opposite lower) and the air pipes can be plainly seen on the right.

Opposite top. ***DB991259 (Taken at Hoo Jct., Spring 1981)***
As well as the DACE opposite, some existing ballast opens were also modernised. DB991259 is a vacuum-braked LAMPREY which has been given new sides. Compare it with the original in Vol. 2, page 93 (upper). This particular vehicle was also originally unfitted and has received both vacuum brakegear and OLEO hydraulic buffers. Livery is Olive Green and, although the ZBV code has been given, there is no name. (Ref: W9796/DL)

Above. ***DB982223 (Taken at Northwich, Summer 1980)*** *To provide the Merseyrail system with some compatible ballast wagons, which could work with modern air braked ballast hoppers, a small number of 12T SOLE wagons were converted. DB982223 is coded ZCA and is in Olive Green livery. The new air brake cylinder is prominent below the solebar. (Ref: W9863/DL)*

Right. ***DB986224 (Taken at South Lambeth, Sum. 1980)*** *A second reason for providing wagons with additional air brakes was an area modernisation scheme, which could be either electrification or re-signalling. Wagons would be required to transport things such as concrete bases for catenary and signal gantries and signal troughing. Invariably, such vehicles were given air brakes so that they could travel in SPEEDLINK services. DB986224, in Olive Green livery and coded ZBQ, is one of these. (Ref: W9606/DL)*

Section 43. P. W. Hopper Wagons (Modern)

DB982637 (Taken at Briton Ferry, 12/3/83)
The SEA LION was the less common design and was not repeated during the second round of 40T hopper building. Thus by the early 1980s, these vehicles were passing through the the workshops for general overhaul and receiving full repaints. This example shown here appears to be one such vehicle, judging by its condition, but, interestingly, it has received Olive Green rather than the new yellow/grey livery.
(Ref: W12776/DL)

In Volume 2, page 91, the first air-braked hoppers, the WHALE and the SEA LION, were studied. The former, built in 1966/67, were air braked only and the latter, which followed in 1971, had both air brakes and vacuum brakes with A.F.I.

A third type was also built in 1971, which were identical to the SEA LION but having air brakes and vacuum through pipes. These vehicles were designated SEA COW and were coded YGB. Numbers were DB982540 to DB982564 and they were built by BREL Shildon to Lot 3724, design code being YG500A. Three extra vehicles, DB982565 to DB982567, were built in the same year to Lot 3777 but no difference can be detected. DB982545 (opposite lower) illustrates the type.

The SEA COW was the preferred design when the next batch of ballast hoppers was selected and, once again, two batches were ordered, there being no obvious changes between either. The main batch, Lot 3966, was split between BREL Ashford and BREL Shildon, and these vehicles were numbered DB980000 to DB980244. The smaller second batch, Lot 4010, was wholly built by BREL Shildon and the numbers were DB980245 to DB980250. All vehicles appeared in 1981/82. These later wagons (above, and opposite upper and centre) had significant differences although the basic shape was the same. All the early bogie hoppers, the WHALE, the SEA LION and the Lots 3724/3777 SEA COW, had bolted bodywork with U-channel vertical bracing. The later SEA COW had welded bodywork. The bogies were modernised to French pattern Y27s and the steps were also changed. Finally, they had protective shields fitted over the end platforms.

DB980038 (Taken at Camberwell, Summer 1981)
This view of a Lot 3966 SEA COW gives a rare look at the top of the air brake cylinder. The vehicle was recorded at a permanent way renewal site in connection with track alterations for the new Victoria panel signal box in South East London. The prominent protective shields on the end platforms are thought to be there to prevent rail staff from accidently getting too close to overhead power supply cables. The standard yellow/grey livery is seen here. Also note the red flag on the next line and the oil lamp beside it. This was how lines blocked by engineer's possession were denoted even in the 1980s. By the next decade, there would be plastic barriers and flashing lights.
(Ref: W9836B/DL)

DB980006 (Taken at Hoo Junction, Summer 1981)
This further view of a Lot 3966 SEA COW shows the opposite end, without the brake equipment. Note that this end also lacks the brake wheel. The first twenty vehicles of Lot 3966 were turned out in a rather unusual livery of white bodywork with wide upper yellow side band, black bogies and black lettering. (Ref: W9835/DL)

DB982545 (Taken at Hoo Junction, Summer 1981)
The first batch of SEA COW hoppers, the 25 vehicles of Lot 3724, were ten years old when this view was taken and, as can be seen, there were quite a few differences. The bogies are the most obvious but the steps over the bogies were also different and there were no overhead shields protecting the platforms. Livery of these at this stage was Olive Green with white lettering.
(Ref: W9846/DL)

Further Research

As in the previous volumes in this series, the author offers a service of further research to any interested readers. The service, which runs on a personal, friendly and non-commercial basis, provides access for individuals to much additional information, data, drawings and individual copies of photographs. It is acknowledged that the requirements of those wishing to make use of this research service will differ greatly and, therefore, the service is very much 'bespoke', being tailored to individual needs. There are three main elements to the research service which were described in detail in volumes 1 and 2. Data sheets can now be provided with accompanying laser printed digital images from original negatives. Although not to full photographic quality, the laser prints provide a sufficiently detailed image suitable for modelling purposes.

The research service is operated on a personal, non-commercial basis and prices will reflect the basic costs incurred on making the information available. For further details on the research service write enclosing a stamped addressed envelope to the author;

David Larkin, 17 Albion Court, Albion Road, Sutton, Surrey, SM2 5TB.

Other titles in this series.

Working Wagons

Volume 1. 1968 - 1973

by David Larkin

ISBN 0 9507960 6 9

The first volume in this series reviews the period when many traditional wagon types, although still in revenue service, were steadily declining and the first batches of modern designs were taking to the rails.

Working Wagons

Volume 2. 1974 - 1979

by David Larkin

ISBN 0 9507960 7 7

This second volume covers that often overlooked but interesting period when many recently rebuilt traditional types could still be seen running alongside the emerging first and second generation air braked designs.

In preparation, the final volume in this series; Working Wagons Volume 4. 1985 to 1991.
The author is also currently researching wagons of the 1950s and 1960s for possible future publication.

Also from Santona Publications, the first ever in-depth modellers guide to the classic diesel and electric age.

Modelling the British Rail Era

by Ian Fleming, Steve Flint, Ken Gibbons and Jeff Taylor.

ISBN 0 9507960 8 5

The British Rail era, from 1964 to 1994, is a fascinating and recent period in our country's railway history, yet it is often overlooked by modellers. This book aims to change that perception and presents a comprehensive review of BR operations examining how they can be readily adapted to create captivating, inspirational and authentic model railways.

Packed with information to help modellers of the period achieve complete historical accuracy, the book also includes a specially chosen selection of prototype plans and modelling tips together with numerous layout themes that are ideally suited to home locations.

All this is rounded off with a focused emphasis on portraying the BR freight scene and even those who are dyed-in-the-wool steam age modellers will find much between these covers that will amaze, enlighten and inspire.

As part of our ongoing book development programme we are keen to hear from potential authors with a particular interest in the British Rail period. Topics related to infrastructure, passenger vehicles and DMUs, freight stock and traffic flows are of especial interest. We are also interested in top quality colour photographs relating directly to these topics, particularly pre-1980. Write in the first instance, enclosing a stamped addressed envelope, to; **Santona Publications, Rydal Mount, 224, Marlborough Avenue, Hull HU5 3LE.**